I0446749

Canon EOS R3 User Reference

A Comprehensive Companion for Mastering the Features and Functions of the EOS R3 Camera

By

Clyde Bertram

Copyright ©2023 Clyde Bertram,

All rights reserved

Table of Content

INTRODUCTION

The Canon EOS R3 is a professional-grade full-frame mirrorless camera that offers a wide range of features and capabilities for both photographers and videographers. It is the flagship of Canon's EOS R series, and it is designed to meet the demands of professional photographers and videographers who need a camera that is both powerful and versatile.

The EOS R3 features a 24.1-megapixel full-frame CMOS sensor that captures stunning high-resolution images with excellent detail and low noise. The camera's dual Pixel CMOS AF system provides fast and accurate autofocus, even in low-light conditions. And its 7.59fps continuous shooting speed lets you capture fast-moving action without missing a beat.

The EOS R3 is also a great choice for videographers. Its 4K UHD 60p video recording capabilities allow you to capture high-quality movies with exceptional detail. And its 5-axis in-body image stabilization ensures that your videos will be smooth and blur-free.

This guide is a comprehensive overview of the Canon EOS R3 camera. It covers everything from how to set up the camera and take your first pictures to more advanced topics like how to use the camera's autofocus system and shoot in manual mode. This guide is written in a simple and easy-to-understand format so that it can be used by beginners and experienced photographers alike.

CHAPTER 1: GETTING THE CAMERA UP AND RUNNING

Preparing the Camera for Initial Use

Attaching the Camera Strap

You've got that awesome new camera you've been dreaming of, and you're eager to start taking pictures. But hold on! Do you know how to correctly put on the camera strap? If you do it wrong, the camera might slip. This camera is pretty heavy, especially with the lens and flash, so it can get quite heavy around your neck.

To make sure you look good with your camera, follow these steps to attach the strap:

1. Put the strap through the metal ring, starting from the outside and moving toward the camera.
2. Slide the strap into the connector, pull it down, and create a loop by pulling a part through the buckle from above.
3. Insert the short part into the buckle's top hole and wrap it inside the loop you made.
4. Thread the short part through the bottom of the buckle, and pull it down between the other strap parts.
5. Pull the long part of the strap up to tighten the slack in the buckle.
6. Slide the clasp up to the buckle; it might be a bit tricky, but it's a one-time effort.
7. Repeat these steps on the other side.

Here, to enable you to focus on taking nice pictures, the camera strap is properly attached to the camera.

Charge the battery

1. Plug the charger into the wall and connect it to the power cable.
2. Take off the protective covers from the charger and battery.
3. Put the battery into any slot on the charger; it will start charging automatically.
4. Wait until all three lights on the charger turn solid green to know the battery is fully charged. The time it takes can vary based on temperature and battery capacity.

The battery can be charged in any of the designated charging slots. The charging process commences automatically upon insertion of the battery, indicated by a flashing or solid green charging indicator light.

A fully charged battery is signified when all three charging lights (50%/80%/100%) illuminate steadily in green. The duration of the charging process is influenced by various factors, including ambient temperature and battery capacity. For instance, charging a completely depleted battery at room temperature (23°C/73°F) typically takes approximately 2 hours and 50 minutes.

Take note: Charging might be slower (up to about 5 hours) when it's cold (5-10°C/41-50°F) for safety.

Inserting/removing batteries

Put a fully charged battery into your camera.

Inserting the battery

1. Ensure that the cover of the battery compartment is taken off.
2. Put the battery in firmly, making sure it goes in all the way.

Removing the battery

Turn the battery release handle to take out the battery. Make sure the power switch is off. Move the handle outward and turn it as shown by the arrow to remove the battery. Always use the provided cover on the battery to avoid short circuits. When not using the camera, put on the cap for the battery compartment.

Insert/remove card

Inserting the card

This camera can use two cards. To record, you need at least one card in the camera. If you have two cards, you can either record to one card or save the same image on both cards simultaneously. Follow these steps:

1. Open the card slot cover (1 & 2).

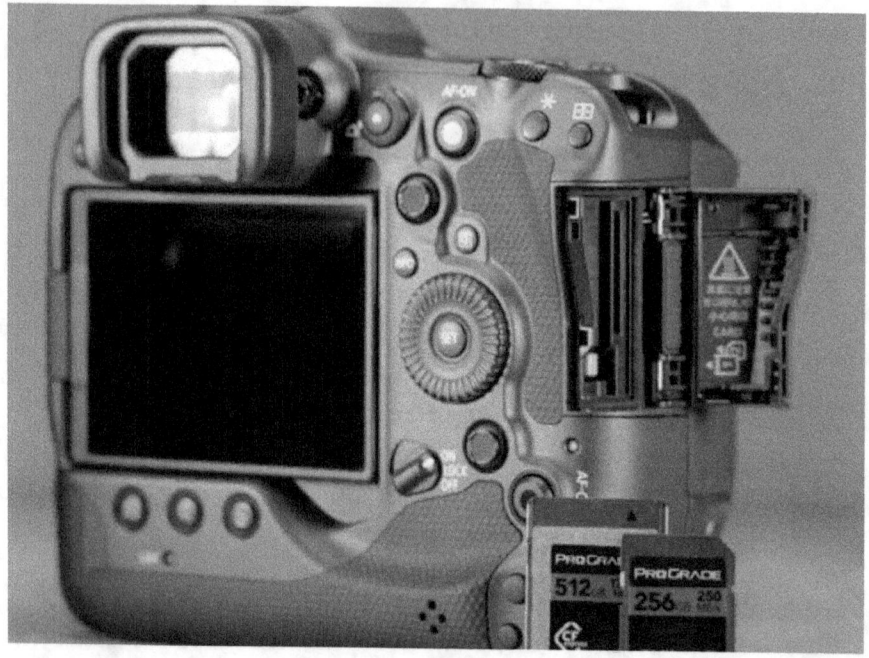

2. Insert the CFexpress card in the back slot and the SD card in the front slot.
   CFexpress card: Put the card with the label towards you into the slot, making sure it goes in the right way to avoid camera damage. Push the grey eject button for Card 1. For the SD card, insert it with the label facing you until it clicks.

3. Close the lid by sliding it in the direction of the arrow until it clicks.
4. Turn on the power switch, and you'll see icons for the inserted cards.

Removing the card

Turn off the power switch. Check that the memory card Access Lamp is not lit before you open the cover. Open the Cover (1 & 2). If you see "Saving" on the screen, keep the cover closed.

Take out the cards. For CFexpress, press the eject button, and for SD cards, gently push and release. Pull the cards straight out, then close the cover.

Wait until the red thermometer icon shows up before taking out the card. The camera gets hot, so turn off the power and wait a bit before removing the card to avoid losing or damaging your pictures. Be cautious when taking the card out.

Switch On the Camera

Flip the power button to turn the camera on. The switch has three positions:

- ON for camera power.
- OFF for turning it off.
- LOCK for activating the camera with the multifunction lock enabled.

When the camera is not in use, set the power switch to the OFF position.

Set the date, time, time zone, and Language

Date/Time/Region

Upon initial usage or whenever the date/time/zone settings are reset, kindly follow the instructions provided below to establish the desired time zone.

Once the initial time zone setup is complete, you can effortlessly modify this setting at any point in the future, and the date/time will automatically adjust accordingly.

Given that the captured image's metadata includes date and time information, ensuring accurate date and time settings is crucial.

1. Access the Settings Menu:
    Click on the Setup Menu icon located on the camera's display.

2. Navigate to Date/Time/Zone Settings:
    From the list of options presented, select Date/Time/Zone.

3. Establish the Time Zone:
    a. Rotate Quick Control Dial: Turn the Quick Control Dial 1 to choose Time Zone.
    b. Confirm Selection: Press the SET button to confirm your selection.
    c. Choose Time Zone: Rotate the Quick Control Dial 1 to scroll through the available time zones.

d. Confirm Time Zone: Once you've located your desired time zone, press the SET button to confirm your selection.

4. Set the Time Difference (if applicable):

    a. Access Time Difference Setting: If your specific time zone isn't listed among the available options, press the MENU button. This will open a more detailed menu.

    b. Navigate to Time Difference: Locate the Time difference option and select it.

    c. Adjust Time Difference: Rotate the Quick Control Dial 1 to adjust the time difference relative to UTC (Coordinated Universal Time).

    d. Confirm Time Difference: Press the SET button to confirm the adjusted time difference.

5. Set the Date and Time:

    a. Select Date Components: Rotate the Quick Control Dial 1 to highlight the desired date component (day, month, or year).

    b. Adjust Date Components: Press the SET button to enter the adjustment mode. Rotate the Quick Control Dial 1 to change the selected date component.

    c. Confirm Date Components: Repeat steps a and b for the remaining date components until the entire date is set accurately.

    d. Set Time Components: Rotate the Quick Control Dial 1 to highlight the desired time component (hour, minute, or second).

    e. Adjust Time Components: Press the SET button to enter the adjustment mode. Rotate the Quick

Control Dial 1 to change the selected time component.

f. Confirm Time Components: Repeat steps d and e for the remaining time components until the entire time is set accurately.

Once you've completed these steps, the camera's date, time, and time zone will be set correctly.

Set daylight saving time (DST)

You have the option to enable or disable Daylight Saving Time (DST) based on your preference. When enabled, the displayed time will be advanced by one hour. To disable DST, rotate the Quick Control Dial 1 to select Daylight Off and press the SET button.

Conversely, to enable DST, rotate the dial to select Daylight and press the SET button. When DST is activated, the time set in step 3 will be adjusted forward by one hour. Conversely, if Daylight Off is selected, DST will be deactivated, and the clock will revert back by one hour.

Complete the settings

Rotate the Quick control dial to choose "OK" and then press the SET button.

Language

1. Locate and click on the Setup Menu icon displayed on the camera's screen.
2. From the list of available options, select Language.

3. Rotate the Quick Control Dial 1 to scroll through the available language options.

4. Once you've identified your preferred language, press the SET button to confirm your selection.

How to connect a RF lens to a Canon camera

Before you can attach a lens to your camera, you'll need to ensure you have the correct type of lens. Lenses are not included with the camera body, so you'll need to purchase one separately. Canon cameras use RF, EF, EF-S, or EF-M lenses. RF lenses do not require an adapter, while EF, EF-S, and EF-M lenses require an adapter to be compatible with the EOS R3.

Additionally, EF-M lenses are not compatible with the EOS R3. Lenses are also categorized as AF-S or AF-I based on their focusing capabilities. Your camera is only capable of automatically focusing on AF-S lenses. Although compatible, the camera can only focus on AF-I lenses manually due to their rarity and high cost. While other types of lenses can be used with the camera, manual focusing will be required.

1. Turn off the camera and remove the cover that covers the lens mount in the front side of the camera.

2. Detach the cover that covers the back of the lens.

3. Hold the lens in front of the camera so that the small red/white dots on the lens match the corresponding dots on the camera body. The terminology for these two white dots is mounting index. When connecting the lens, adjust the markings.

4. Place the lens on your camera's lens mount, ensuring the dots remain aligned.
5. After doing this, grab the back collar of the lens (i.e. the side that does not move, not the front end of the lens barrel that's movable).
6. Rotate the lens in anticlockwise direction until it snaps into place. That is, rotate it to the side of your camera where the shutter button is located as shown by arrow in the diagram.
7. Push the Focus mode Switch on the lens to AF. AF: Abbreviation for Auto Focus. MF: Abbreviation for manual focus. Autofocus doesn't work when the switch is set to MF. If your RF lens doesn't have a focus mode switch, select the AF menu in your camera menus, choose Focus Mode and set the focus mode to [AF] or [MF].
8. Remove the front lens cover.
9. If your lens has an aperture ring, set the ring and lock it so that the maximum possible f-stop number is gotten for the aperture.

Look at the lens manual to find out if the lens has a lens aperture ring and how to fix it.

Even though your camera has a system to reduce dust, it's better to attach or switch the lens in a clean place. For instance, avoid doing it at the beach to prevent dust, sand, or dirt from getting in. Also, when attaching the lens, point the camera down to stop particles from falling in.

How to remove the camera lens

1. First, turn off your camera.

2. Look for the lens release button, usually marked with an arrow.
3. Press the lens release button and twist the lens clockwise until it lines up with the camera body.
4. Put the back protection cover on the lens.
5. If you're not adding another lens right away, use the camera safety cap to cover the lens mount.

How to connect an EF/EF-S lens to a Canon camera

1. Turn off the camera and open the front cover.
2. Ensure the back cover of the lens is taken off.
3. Put the lens on the adapter, matching the red or white marks.
4. Connect the adapter to the camera, aligning the red marks.
5. Place the adapter on the camera's lens mount, keeping the dots in line.
6. Hold the back part of the lens (the part that doesn't move) by the collar.
7. Turn the lens counterclockwise until it clicks into place, pointing towards the side of your camera with the shutter button.
8. Switch the lens Focus mode to AF, which stands for Auto Focus. Make sure it's not on MF (Manual Focus) because Auto Focus won't work in that mode.
9. Take off the front lens cover.
10. If your lens has an aperture ring, adjust and lock it to the highest f-stop number. Check your lens manual to find the ring and learn how to secure it.

Remove the lens

1. Push the lens release button and turn the adapter as shown by the arrow.
2. Turn the lens until it won't turn anymore, then take it off.
3. Take the lens off the adapter. Hold the lens release lever, turn the lens counterclockwise until it stops, and then take it off. Put the lens cap on the removed lens.

Exploring External Camera Features

Topside controls

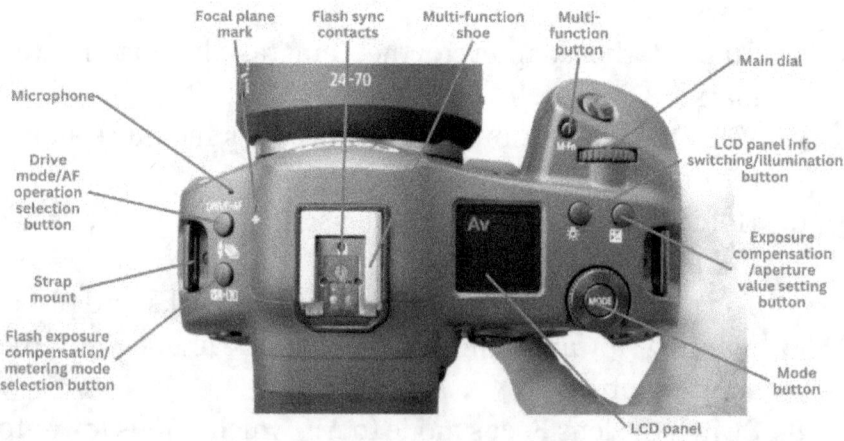

LCD panel: The LCD panel is a 4.1-inch high-resolution touchscreen that displays the camera's settings and menus. You can also use the touchscreen to control the camera's functions, such as focusing and setting the aperture and shutter speed.

Microphone: The microphone is used to record sound when you are shooting videos. You can adjust the microphone level in the camera's settings menu.

Drive mode or AF operation selection button: This button is used to select the drive mode and AF operation. The drive mode determines how many frames the camera will shoot per second, while the AF operation determines how the camera will focus on your subject.

Strap mount: The strap mount is used to attach the camera strap. The strap helps to keep the camera secure when you are shooting.

Flash exposure compensation or metering mode selection button: This button is used to adjust the flash exposure compensation or to select the metering mode. The flash exposure compensation controls how much light the flash will add to your photo, while the metering mode determines how the camera will measure the light in your scene.

Multi-function shoe: The multi-function shoe is used to attach accessories, such as an external flash or an electronic viewfinder.

Flash sync contacts: The flash sync contacts are used to connect the camera to an external flash.

Quick control dial 2: The quick control dial 2 is used to adjust the camera's settings quickly and easily. You can assign different functions to the dial, such as adjusting the aperture or shutter speed.

Mode button: The mode button is used to select the camera's shooting mode. There are a variety of shooting modes to choose from, including manual, aperture priority, shutter priority, and program.

Exposure compensation or Aperture Value Setting button: This button is used to adjust the exposure compensation or to set the aperture value. The exposure compensation controls how much lighter or darker the camera will make the image, while the aperture value controls the amount of light that enters the lens.

LCD panel info witching or illumination button: This button is used to cycle through the different information displays on the LCD panel. You can also use this button to turn on or off the LCD panel's backlight.

Main dial: The main dial is used to adjust the camera's settings. You can rotate the dial to change the shutter speed, aperture, or ISO.

Shutter button: The shutter button is used to take a picture. When you press the shutter button, the camera will open the shutter and let light into the sensor.

Multi-function button: The multi-function button is a programmable button that can be assigned to a variety of functions. You can assign functions to the button, such as setting the white balance or activating the self-timer.

Front features

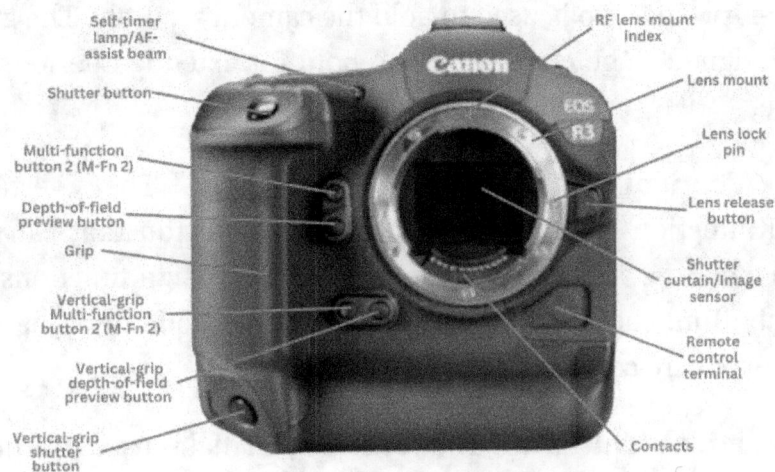

1. Self-timer lamp or AF-assist beam: The self-timer lamp is used to indicate when the self-timer is active. The AF-assist beam is used to help the camera focus in low-light conditions.

2. Shutter button: The shutter button is used to take a picture. When you press the shutter button, the camera will open the shutter and let light into the sensor.

3. Multifunction button 2 (or M-Fn 2): The multifunction button 2 is a programmable button that can be assigned to a variety of functions. You can assign functions to the button, such as adjusting the white balance or activating the self-timer.

4. Depth of field preview button: The depth of field preview button is used to preview the depth of field of your photo. When you press the button, the camera will stop down the lens to show you how much of your scene will be in focus.

5. Grip: The grip is used to hold the camera securely. The grip is designed to be comfortable to hold for extended periods of time.

6. Vertical Multifunction button: The vertical multifunction button is a programmable button that can be assigned to a variety of functions. You can assign functions to the button, such as changing the shooting mode or adjusting the exposure compensation.

7. Vertical Main dial: The vertical main dial is used to adjust the camera's settings. You can rotate the dial to change the shutter speed, aperture, or ISO.

8. Vertical shutter button: The vertical shutter button is used to take a picture when the camera is held in portrait orientation. This is useful for situations where you want to shoot in portrait orientation without having to reconfigure your grip.

9. Mount index for RF lens: The mount index for RF lenses is used to align the lens with the camera body. The mount index is a small red dot on the lens and a small white dot on the camera body.

10. Lens mount: The lens mount is the connection point between the lens and the camera body. The lens mount is designed to hold the lens securely in place.

11. Lens lock pin: The lens lock pin is used to lock the lens in place on the camera body. This prevents the lens from accidentally being removed from the camera.

12. Lens release button: The lens release button is used to release the lens from the camera body. When you press the button, the lens will unlock and you can remove it from the camera.

13. Shutter curtain or Image sensor: The shutter curtain is used to control the amount of light that reaches the image sensor. The image sensor is the part of the camera that captures the image.

14. Remote control terminal: The remote control terminal is used to connect the camera to a remote control. This allows you to control the camera without having to touch it.

15. Contacts: The contacts are used to connect the camera to accessories, such as an external flash or an electronic viewfinder.

16. Vertical depth of field preview button: The vertical depth of field preview button is used to preview the depth of field of your photo when the camera is held in portrait orientation.

17. Vertical Multifunction button 2 (M-Fn 2): The vertical multifunction button 2 is a programmable button that can be assigned to a variety of functions. You can assign functions to the button, such as changing the shooting mode or adjusting the exposure compensation.

18. External microphone IN terminal: The external microphone IN terminal is used to connect an external microphone to the camera. This allows you to record high-quality audio with your videos.

19. Digital terminal: The digital terminal is used to connect the camera to a computer. This allows you to transfer images and videos from the camera to your computer.

20. HDMI micro OUT terminal: The HDMI micro OUT terminal is used to connect the camera to an HDMI-compatible television or monitor. This allows you to view your images and videos on a larger screen.

21. Headphone terminal: The headphone terminal is used to connect headphones to the camera. This allows you to monitor the audio recording of your videos.

22. Ethernet RJ-45 terminal: The Ethernet RJ-45 terminal is a wired network connection port that allows the camera to connect to a computer network. This allows you to transfer images and videos from the camera to a computer or to a network storage device. The Ethernet RJ-45 terminal supports Gigabit Ethernet, which provides a fast and reliable connection for transferring large files

23. PC terminal: The PC terminal is used to connect the camera to a computer using a USB cable. This allows you to transfer images and videos from the camera to your computer.

24. Terminal cover: The terminal cover is used to protect the terminals when they are not in use. The terminal cover is designed to be easy to open and close.

25. Battery: The battery is the power source for the camera. The battery is designed to provide enough power for a full day of shooting.

26. Battery release handle: The battery release handle is used to remove the battery from the camera. The battery release handle is designed to be easy to grip and operate.

Back-of-the-body controls

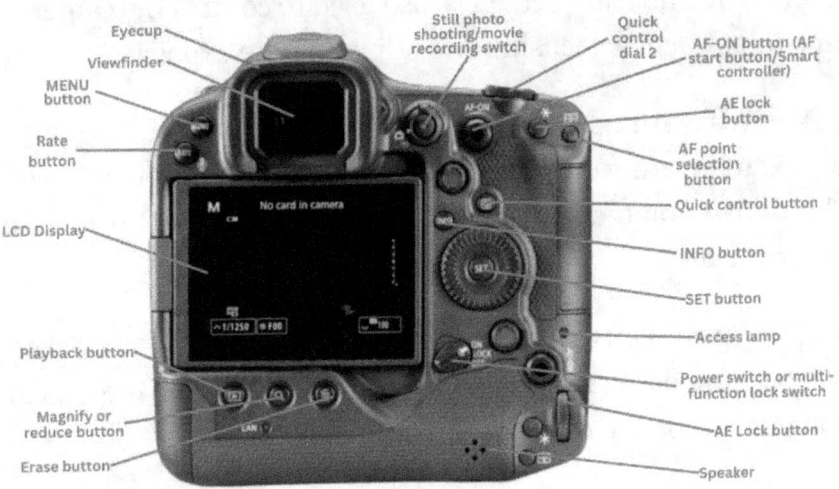

1. Eyecup: The eyecup is a rubber cup that fits around the viewfinder eyepiece. The eyecup helps to block out ambient light and to keep the viewfinder comfortable to use.

2. Menu button: The menu button is used to access the camera's menus. The menus allow you to adjust the camera's settings, such as the shooting mode, focus mode, and white balance.

3. Rating or voice memo button: This button is used to rate images or to record voice memos. The rating function allows you to assign a rating to an image, from one to five stars. This can be helpful for organizing your images. The voice memo function allows you to record a short audio clip with an image.

4. Shooting Screen: The Shooting Screen is a high-resolution LCD display that shows you what the camera is seeing. The Shooting Screen is also used to control the camera's functions, such as focusing and adjusting the exposure.

5. Magnify or reduce button: The magnify or reduce button is used to magnify or reduce the image on the Shooting Screen. This allows you to zoom in on details or to zoom out to see the entire image.

6. Playback button: The playback button is used to enter playback mode. Playback mode allows you to view the images and videos you have taken.

7. Network lamp: The network lamp indicates the status of the camera's network connection. The network lamp will blink when the camera is connected to a network.

8. Erase button: The erase button is used to erase images or videos. The erase button is designed to prevent accidental deletion of images or videos.

9. Power switch or multi-function lock switch: The power switch is used to turn the camera on or off. The multi-function lock switch is used to lock the camera's controls. This prevents accidental changes to the camera's settings.

10. Speaker: The speaker is used to play back audio recordings. The speaker is also used to play sound effects, such as the shutter sound.

11. AF point selection button (vertical grip): The AF point selection button is used to select the autofocus point. This allows you to control where the camera focuses.

12. AE lock button (Vertical-grip): The AE lock button is used to lock the exposure. This prevents the camera's exposure from changing when you recompose the shot.

13. Quick control dial 2 (Vertical-grip): The quick control dial 2 is used to adjust the camera's settings. You can rotate the dial to change the shutter speed, aperture, or ISO.

14. AF start button or Smart controller (Vertical-grip): The AF start button is used to start autofocus. The Smart controller is used to control the camera's functions, such as focusing and adjusting the exposure.

15. Access lamp: The access lamp indicates when the camera is accessing the memory card. The access lamp will blink when the camera is reading or writing to the memory card.

16. Multi-controller(Vertical-grip): The multi-controller is used to navigate through the camera's menus. The multi-controller can also be used to control the camera's functions, such as selecting autofocus points and adjusting the exposure.

17. Set button: The set button is used to confirm your settings. The set button is also used to enter or exit menus and submenus.

18. Quick control dial 1: The quick control dial 1 is used to adjust the camera's settings. You can rotate the dial to change the shutter speed, aperture, or ISO.

19. Quick Control button: The Quick Control button is used to access the Quick Control menu. The Quick Control menu allows you to quickly adjust the camera's most frequently used settings.

20. Multi-controller: The multi-controller is used to navigate through the camera's menus. The multi-controller can also be used to control the camera's functions, such as selecting autofocus points and adjusting the exposure.

21. Info button: The info button is used to display additional information about the current camera settings. The info button can also be used to cycle through different information displays.

22. AF point selection button: The AF point selection button is used to select the autofocus point. This allows you to control where the camera focuses.

23. AE lock button: The AE lock button is used to lock the exposure. This prevents the camera's exposure from changing when you recompose the shot.

24. AF start button or Smart controller: The AF start button is used to start autofocus. The Smart controller is used to control the camera's functions, such as focusing and adjusting the exposure.

25. Movie shooting button: The movie shooting button is used to start recording a video. The movie shooting button is also used to stop recording a video.

26. Still photo shooting/movie recording switch: The still photo shooting/movie recording switch is used to switch between still photo mode and movie recording mode.

27. Dioptric adjustment knob: The dioptric adjustment knob is used to adjust the viewfinder's diopter. This allows you to fine-tune the viewfinder's focus so that you can see clearly through it.

28. Viewfinder eyepiece: The viewfinder eyepiece is used to view the image through the viewfinder. The viewfinder eyepiece is also used to protect the viewfinder from dust and scratches.

CHAPTER 2: CONTROLLING FOCUS

In photography, the focus is the clearest part of the picture. It's where the camera lens highlights things, like people or objects. Focus, along with ISO, aperture, and shutter speed, is crucial for good photos. It's important to understand and use it effectively.

Focus Mode

You can make your camera focus automatically (AF or autofocus) or manually (MF). In auto mode, the camera does it for you, adjusting focus based on light. In manual mode, you do it yourself by turning a dial until the image looks clear. How you pick the focus mode depends on the lens you're using.

For RF lenses with a focus mode switch

Just move the lens focus switch to MF (Manual Focus). If your lens has its switch, the camera's switch won't work.

For RF lenses without a focus mode switch:

Press MENU to go back to the Menus screen. Turn the Quick control dial to pick the AF menu tab. Select AF tab 1. Pick Focus mode and press SET. Now, choose between MF or AF.

AF operations

There are two types of AF (auto-focus) that work well in different situations. One-shot AF is great for still subjects, while Servo AF is perfect for capturing moving subjects.

Use the instructions above to change your camera's focus mode to AF.

Press MENU to go back to the Menus screen. Turn the Quick Control dial 2 to pick the AF menu tab. Choose AF tab 1. Pick Focus operation and press SET.

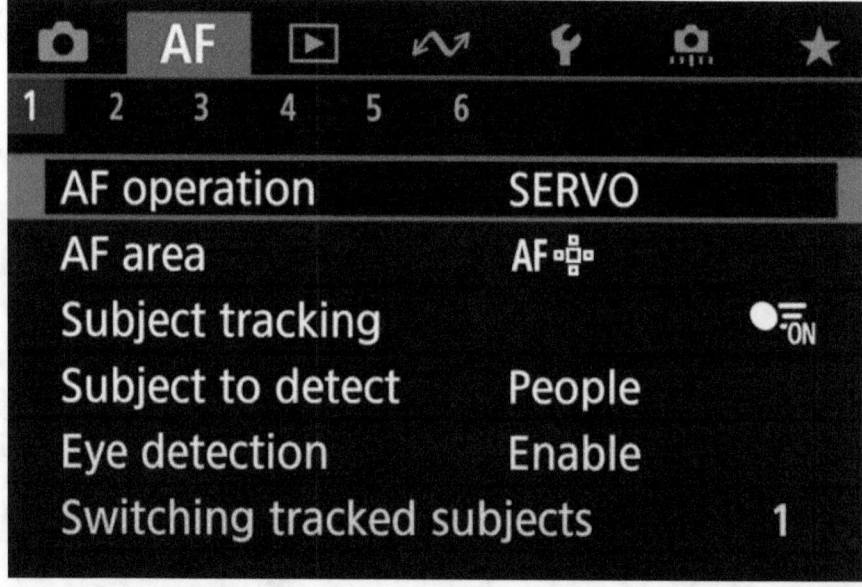

Turn the Quick control dial to pick ONE SHOT or SERVO, then press the SET button.

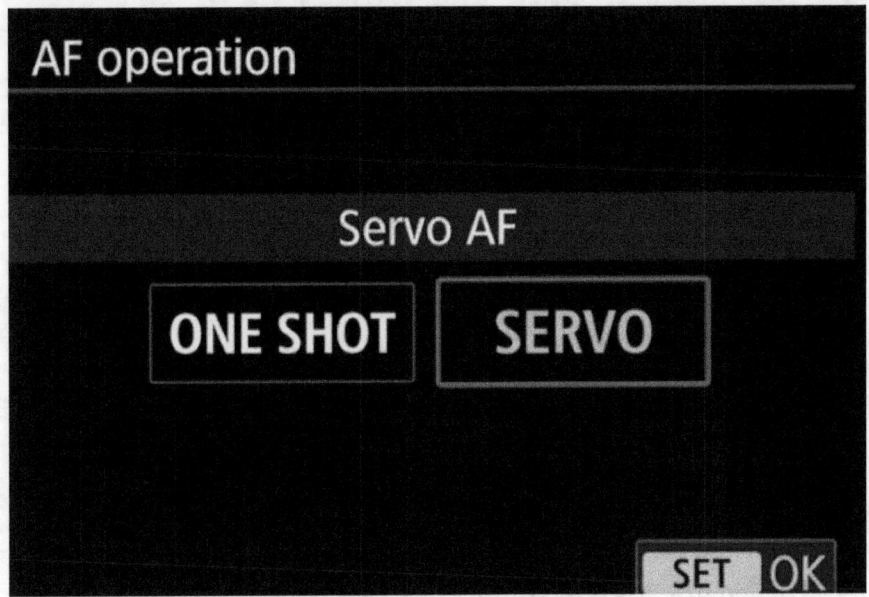

One Shot AF for Stills

This auto-focus works well for pictures. When you press the shutter button halfway, the camera focuses and beeps when it's ready. The green frame means it's focused. Keep the button halfway to lock focus, and you can recompose the shot before taking the picture.

Servo AF for a subject that's moving

This camera function works well for things that are moving. It keeps focusing on the subject when you press the shutter button halfway. When the subject is focused, the focusing frame turns blue. The camera doesn't make a beep when it's focused, and the exposure is set when you take the picture.

Focus Lock

For beginners, it's crucial to learn about Focus Lock, a key setting in photography. It helps focus on subjects that are challenging for the camera's autofocus. Focus lock uses One-Shot AF with a fixed point and readjusts the image before taking a shot.

What does focus lock involve?

Putting your main subject away from the center makes your picture look better. Just make sure your camera is focused on that spot, not the middle. If not, your subject might be blurry while the background stays sharp. To avoid this, use a focus lock, especially for still subjects.

Why is this so important?

Focus lock is a useful trick when you're moving your subject around in the frame. It helps keep your subject clear without worrying about blur, as long as it stays at the same distance from you. This is handy for cameras with fewer focus points, letting you position your subject where there's no specific focus point available.

How do you use it?

To take a picture, choose One-Shot AF mode on your camera. Center your subject in the frame, and press the shutter button halfway to focus. Keep the button half-pressed as you move the subject's position. Maintain a consistent distance from your subject. Once you're happy with the setup, press the shutter button all the way to capture the picture.

Follow these steps to take a photo:

1. Point the white square at your subject and press the shutter button halfway.
2. When the square turns green, press the shutter button halfway again.
3. Compose your shot.
4. Press the shutter button all the way to take the photo.

AF area

If you choose autofocus on your camera, it automatically focuses on things in your picture without much effort from you. However, it might not focus on exactly what you want. It tends to focus on the closest or most detailed part of the image. To change the focus area, you need to adjust the autofocus area (AF-area) mode.

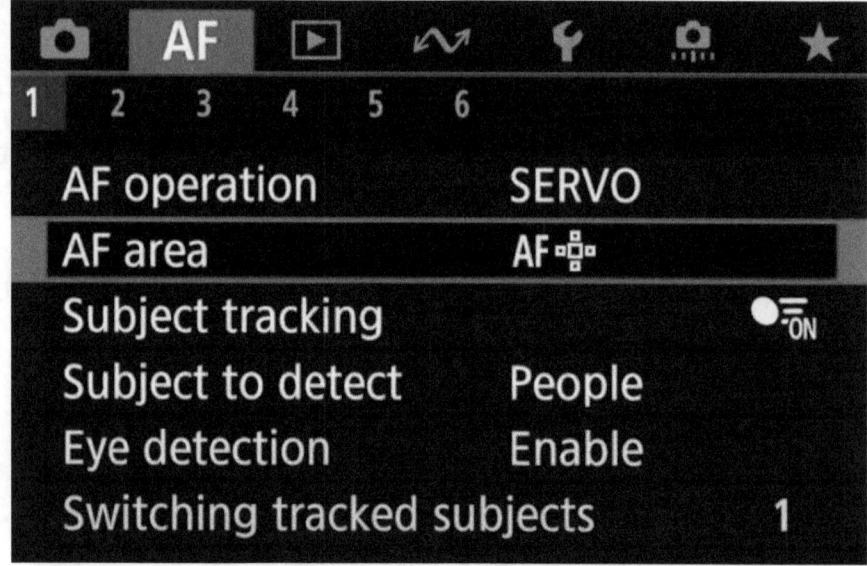

How to Select the AF Area

Pick where your camera focuses based on what you're taking a picture of and the shooting conditions.

To do this:

1. Press MENU on your camera.
2. Turn the Quick Control dial 2 to select the AF menu.
3. Use the Main dial to choose AF tab 1.
4. Turn Quick control dial 1 to pick the AF area and press SET.

Now, choose your AF area:

1. Turn Quick control dial 1 to select an AF area.
2. Press SET.

Canon cameras have 8 different autofocus areas, each shown with its icon.

- **Spot AF:** It hones in on a smaller area compared to single-point autofocus.

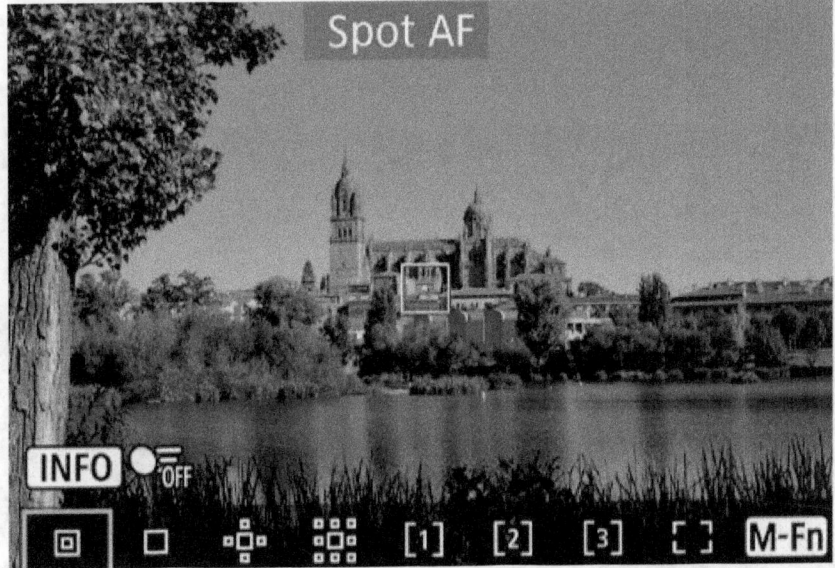

- **1-point AF:** Your camera will focus using just one point.

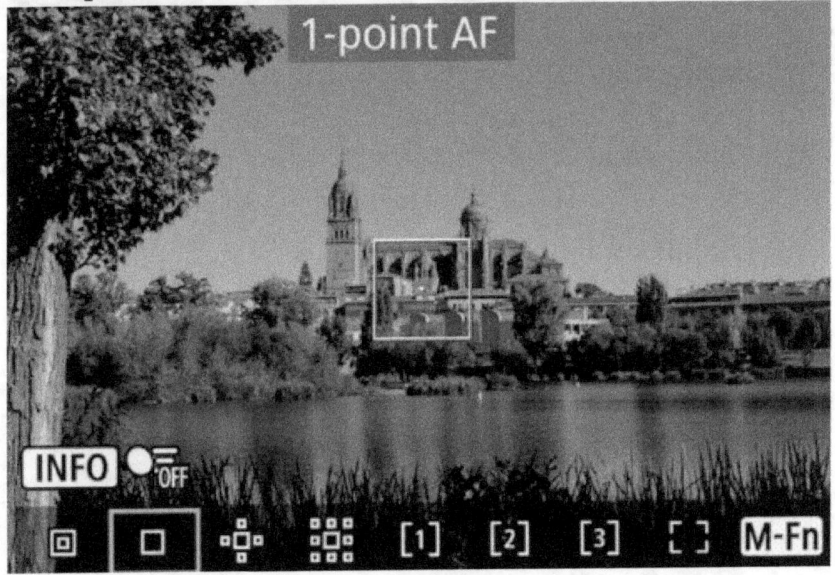

- **Expanded AF area:** Use the blue-boxed AF area for better focus on fast-moving subjects. It's especially helpful for subjects that are hard to track with a single point. When using Servo AF, start by focusing on the 1-point AF.

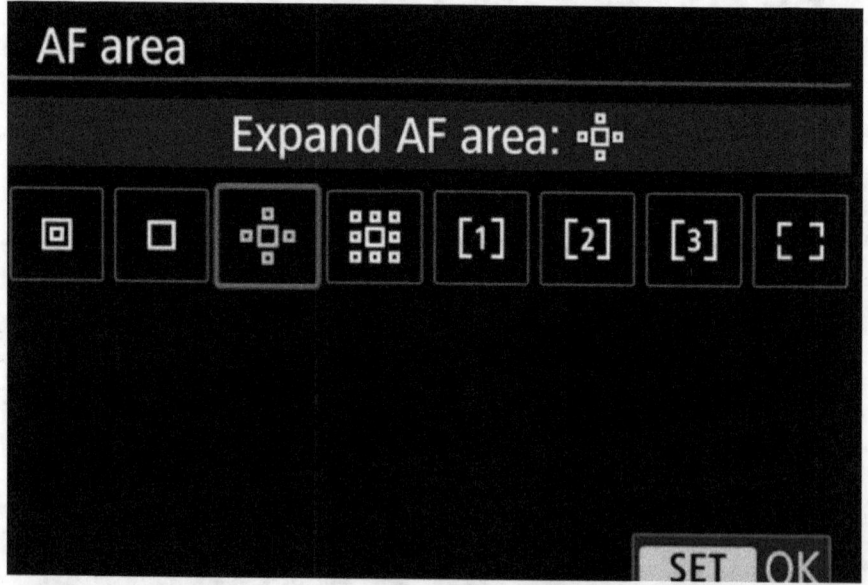

- **Expanded AF area: Around:** Use just one focus point [AF point] and the blue-outlined area around it. This area is larger than the Expanded AF area. When using Servo AF, start by focusing on the single AF point [1-point AF].

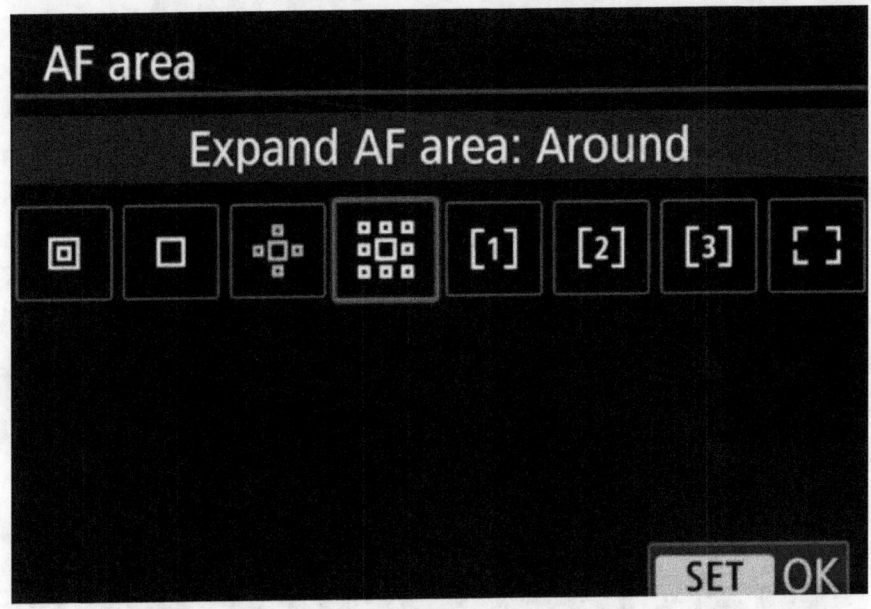

- **Flexible AF zone 1:** The camera starts with a square focus area frame.

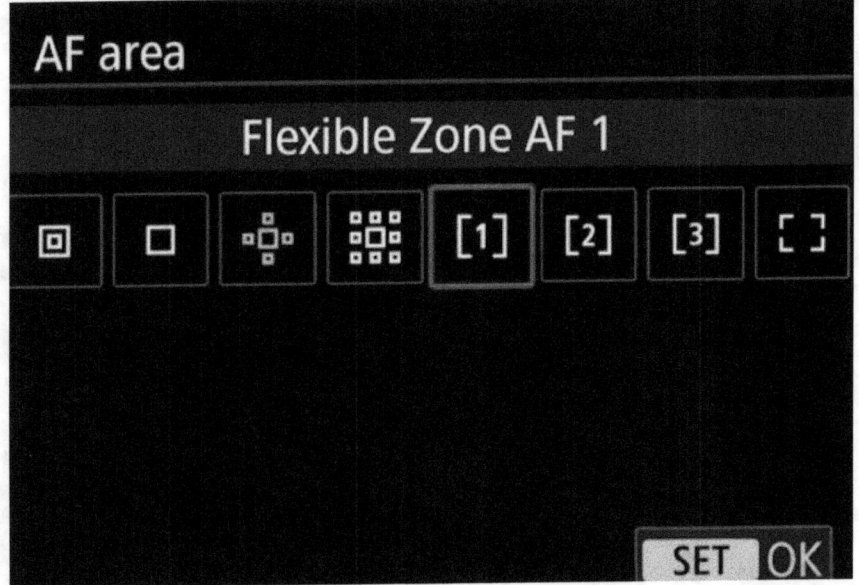

- **Flexible AF Zone 2:** By default, the camera focuses on a rectangular area in the middle of the frame.

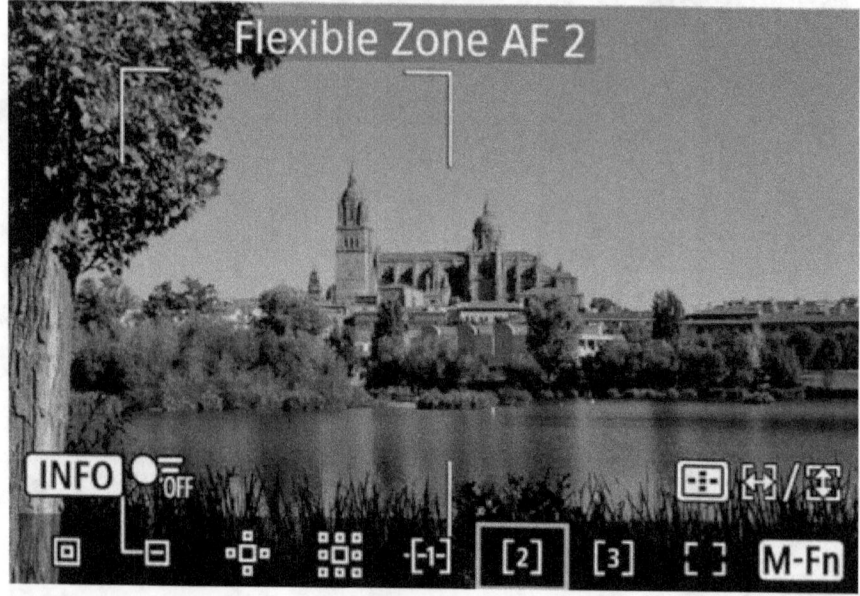

- **Flexible AF Zone 3:** The camera is initially set to focus on a wide horizontal area.

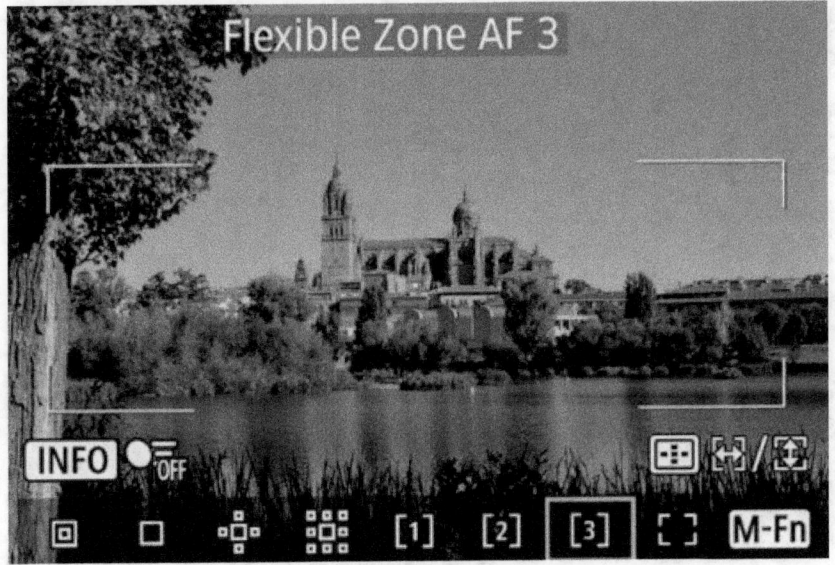

You can change the focus area size with Flexible Zone AF 1-3. It's better for moving things and considers different conditions like faces, vehicles, and subject movement. When you half-press the shutter button, a box shows up above the focus point.

- **Whole area AF:** Auto Select AF with Whole Area AF is better for focusing because it covers a larger area than Flexible Zone AF. This makes it easier to focus, especially for subjects in motion.

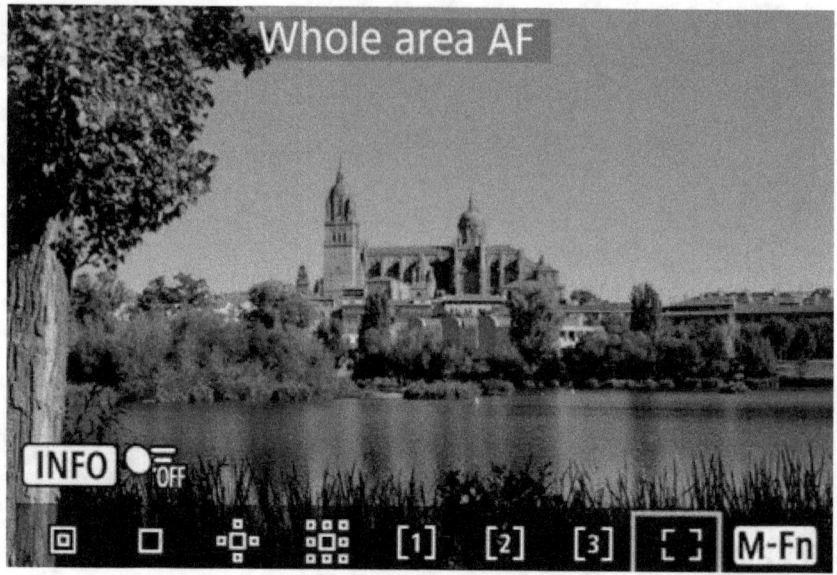

The camera decides where to focus by considering different things like close objects, faces (both people and animals), vehicles, how things are moving, and how far away the subject is. When you press the shutter button halfway, a box shows up at the point where the camera is focusing.

Subject tracking

Subject tracking is great for beginners because it helps you focus on a moving subject. When using it, the camera puts a frame around the main subject, and as the subject moves, the frame follows it.

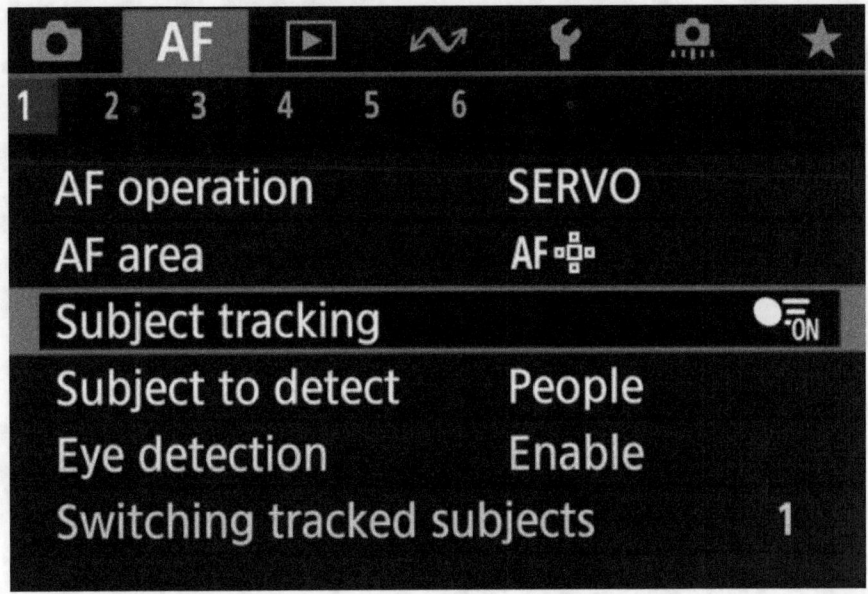

To use Subject tracking, press the MENU button, go to the AF menu tab by rotating the Quick control dial 2, choose AF tab 1 by rotating the Main dial, select Subject tracking by rotating the Quick control dial 1, and press the SET button.

Twist the Quick control dial 1 until you reach ON, then press the SET button.

Subject tracking might not be effective if your subject blends with the background is too big or small, too dark or bright, moves too quickly, or is hidden by other objects.

Manual selection of subject to focus

Examine the tracking frame

Your camera puts a square around things it sees. If the square is not on a specific point, it's gray. When the thing comes close to a point, the square turns white, and you can choose it as the main thing. The point becomes gray. This doesn't happen when recording a movie.

Focus and begin recording/shooting

When you press the shutter button halfway and the camera focuses on the subject, a green frame appears with a beep. If the camera can't focus, you'll see an orange point.

Subject to Detect

You can choose rules to pick the main thing to follow automatically.

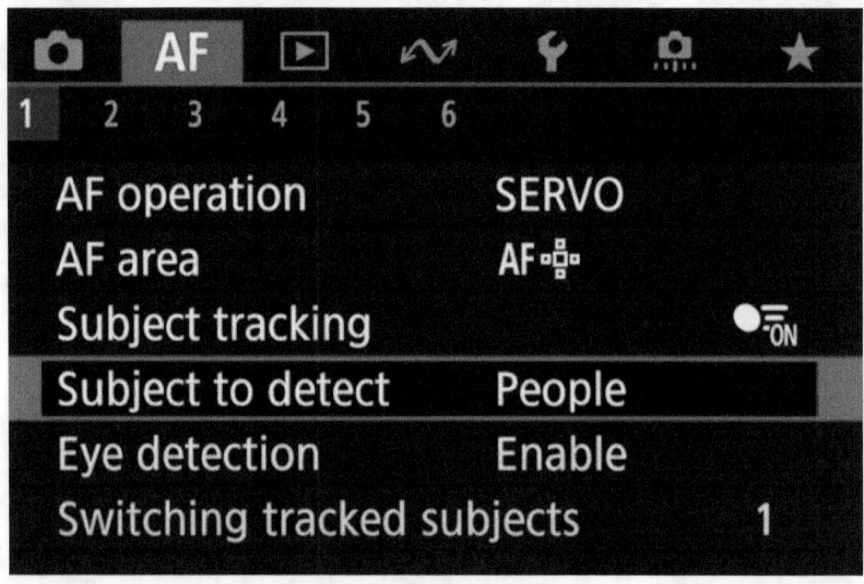

Press the MENU button on your camera to open the menus. Turn the Quick Control dial 2 to select the AF menu tab. Use the Main dial to choose AF tab 1. Turn Quick control dial 1 to pick "Subject to Detect," then press the SET button.

Turn the Quick control dial to pick a subject type, then press the SET button.

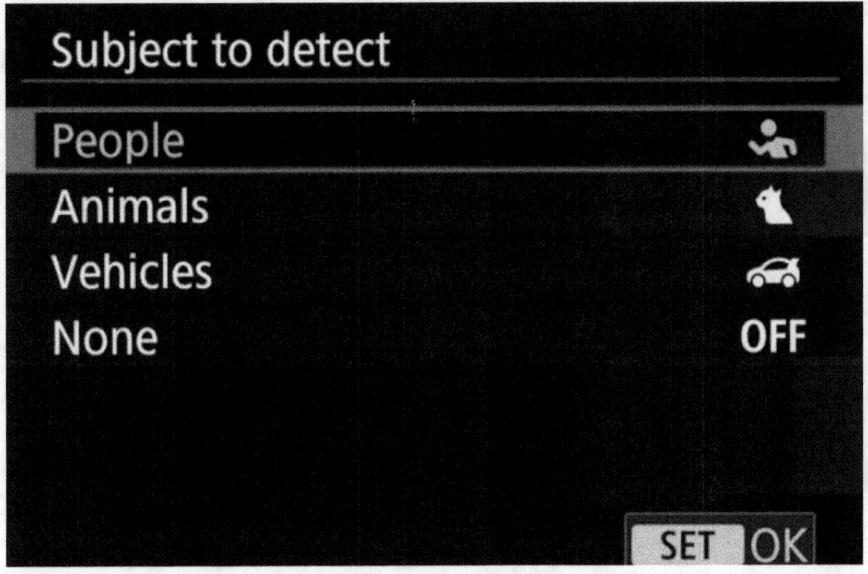

- **People:** The camera first looks for a person's face or head. If it can't find those, it tries to recognize and follow the body. If even the body is hard to identify, the camera might track other body parts.
- **Animal:** The camera finds animals like dogs, cats, and birds, as well as people. It gives more importance to spotting animals. For animals, it looks for faces or bodies, showing a frame around each face it finds. If it

can't recognize the face or body, it might track other parts of the animal's body.

- **Vehicle:** It finds bikes, cars, and people in motorsports, giving more focus to vehicles. The camera aims to spot key details of the whole vehicle, showing a tracking frame. If it can't detect those, it tracks other parts. Press INFO to turn on or off spot detection for basic vehicle info.
- **None:** If the camera can't find a specific subject, it figures out the main thing in the picture by looking at how everything is arranged. There won't be any highlighted tracking frames.

Eye Detection

Capture photos by concentrating on the eyes of people or animals.

Go to your camera settings, select the autofocus menu, go to the first tab, choose Eye Detection, and press the SET button.

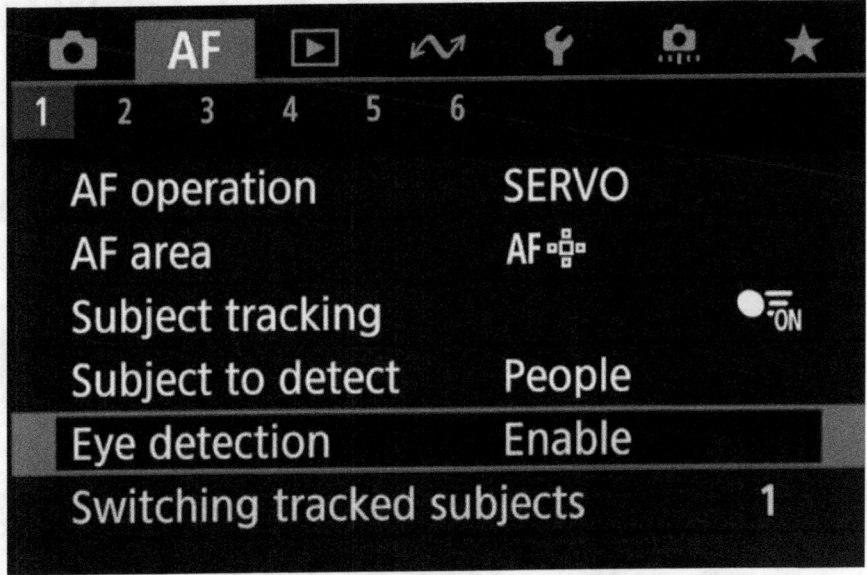

Turn the Quick control dial to select "Enable" and then press the SET button.

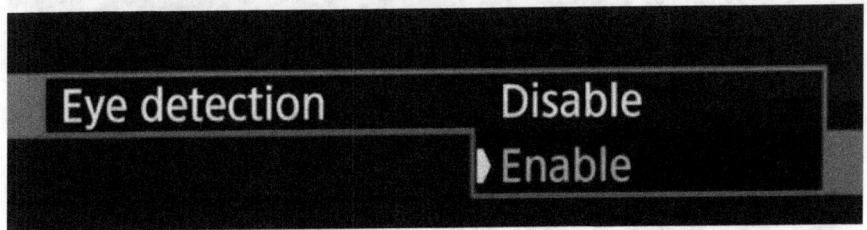

A box shows up around your subject's eye to keep track of it.

When using Whole Area AF, touch the screen or use the Multi-controller to choose the eye you want to focus on. If you use the Multi-controller, the tracking frame becomes Subject Tracking.

You can also pick eyes by tapping the screen in Whole Area AF or during tracking. If the chosen eye isn't detected, it automatically switches to another eye for focus. To take a picture, press the shutter button down.

MF Peaking

Colored outlines help you see the edges of focused things, making it easier to focus. You can change the color and how well it detects edges with MF peaking.

Press the MENU button to open your camera settings. Turn the Quick control dial to select the AF menu. Pick AF tab 5, choose MF peaking settings, and press SET.

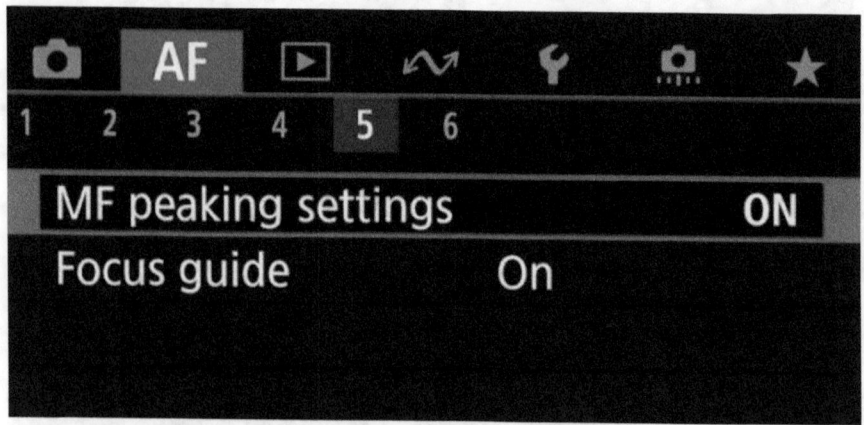

Now, select "Peaking."

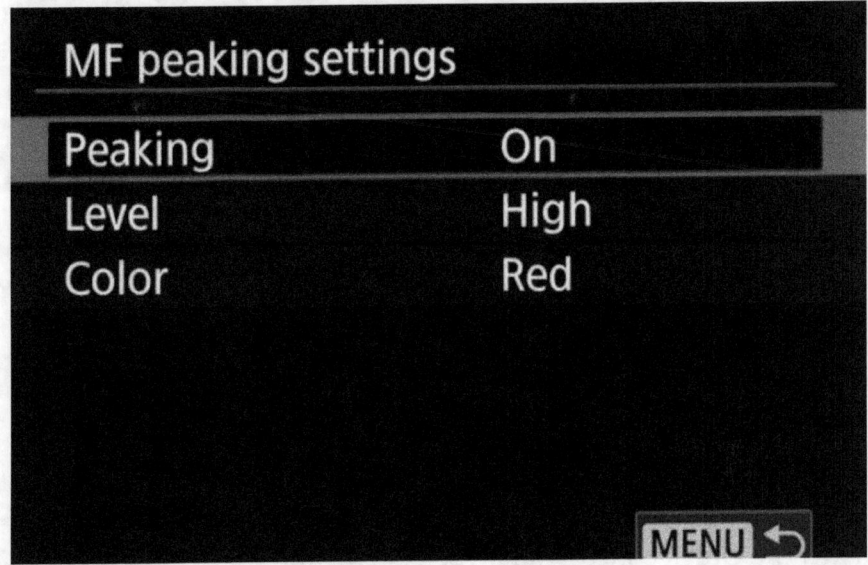

Turn it on.

Adjust the Level and Color options the way you want.

Focus Guide

When you turn on Focus Guide, a frame shows up to tell you where to focus and how much to adjust. Follow these steps to activate the Focus Guide:

Press the MENU button to open your camera settings. Turn the Quick Control dial 2 to select the AF menu.

Go to AF tab 5, pick Focus Guide, and press the SET button.

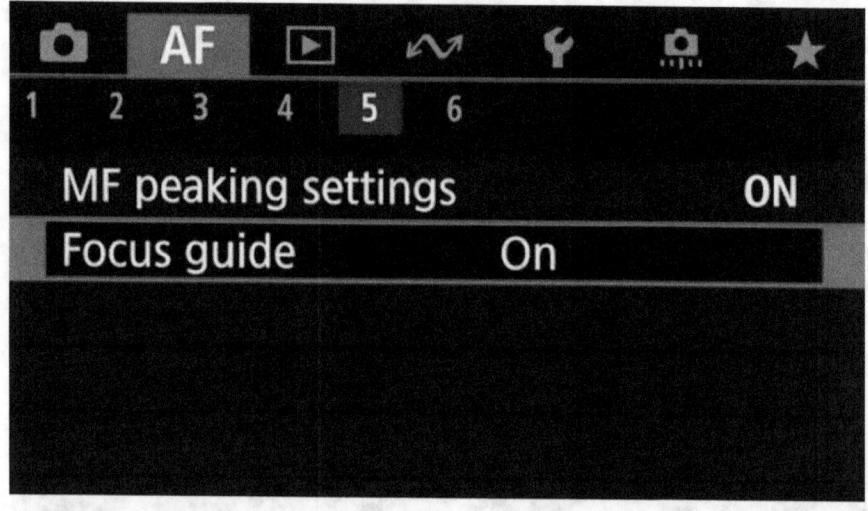

Turn the Quick control dial to select On, and then press the SET button.

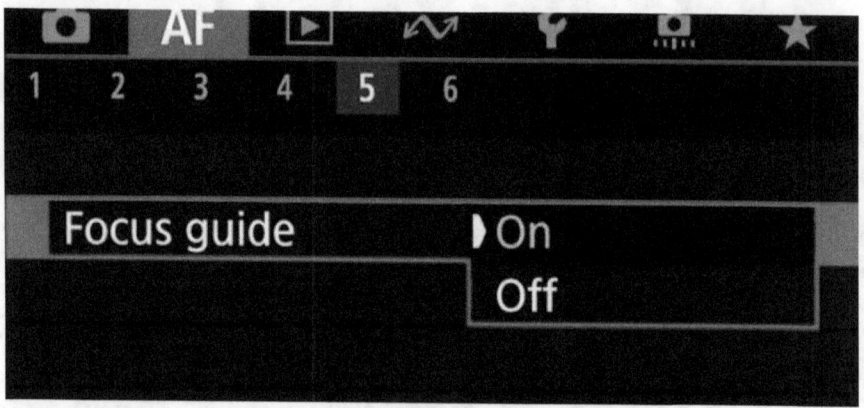

Press MENU to return to the shooting screen. A frame will appear around the face of the main person identified.

To show a guide near the person's eyes in a photo, turn on Subject Tracking and Eye Detection. Press the AF point selection button, use the Multi-controller to move the guide, and press SET to lock it. You can also tap the screen to move and adjust the guide.

Touch or click in the middle of the Multi-controller to center the frame.

Drive Mode

A Drive mode helps you control when your camera takes pictures after you press the button. The Canon EOS R3 has different drive modes, like single shot or continuous shooting. Pick the one that fits your surroundings. To set it up, just look at your camera screen and hold the DRIVE-AF button for 6 seconds.

Turn the Quick control dial 1 to pick a driving mode.

Turn the Quick control dial 2 to choose one of these options. You can select from the available Drive Modes below.

✓   Single Shooting: If you fully press the picture button, only one photo will be taken.

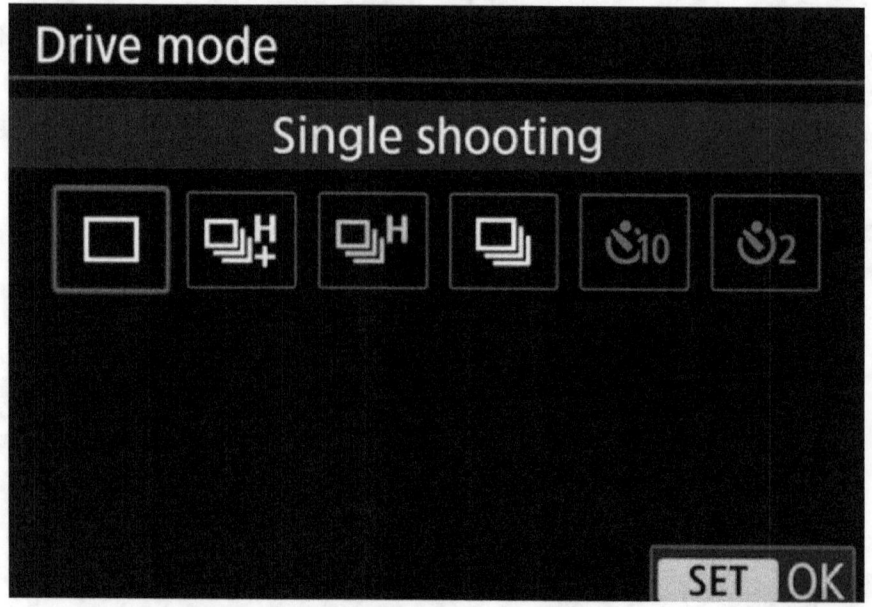

✓   High-speed continuous shooting+: Depending on how you set the shutter mode, you can keep taking pictures by holding down the shutter button.

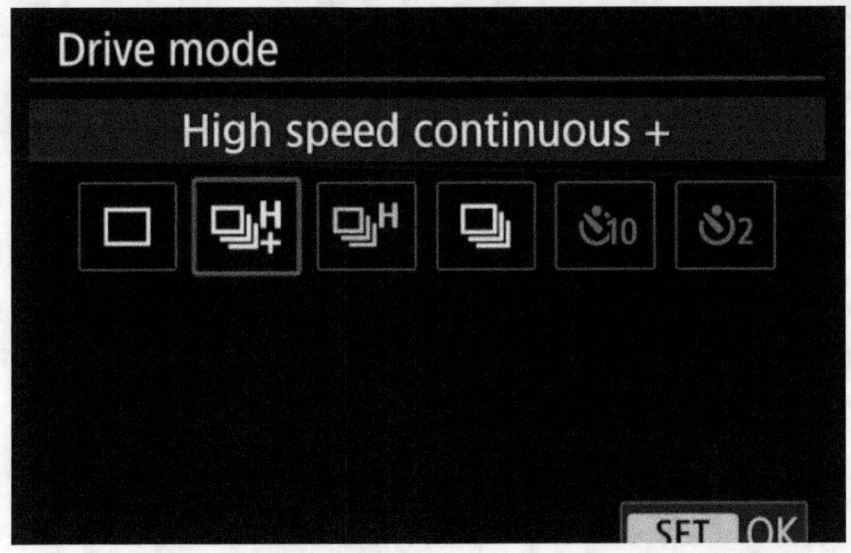

- Mechanical: Maximum of about 15 shots per second
- Electrical first curtain: You can take up to 15 shots per second with a regular camera, but with an electronic one, you can take about 30 shots per second.

✓ High-speed continuous shooting: Depending on how you set the Shutter mode, you can keep taking pictures by holding down the shutter button.

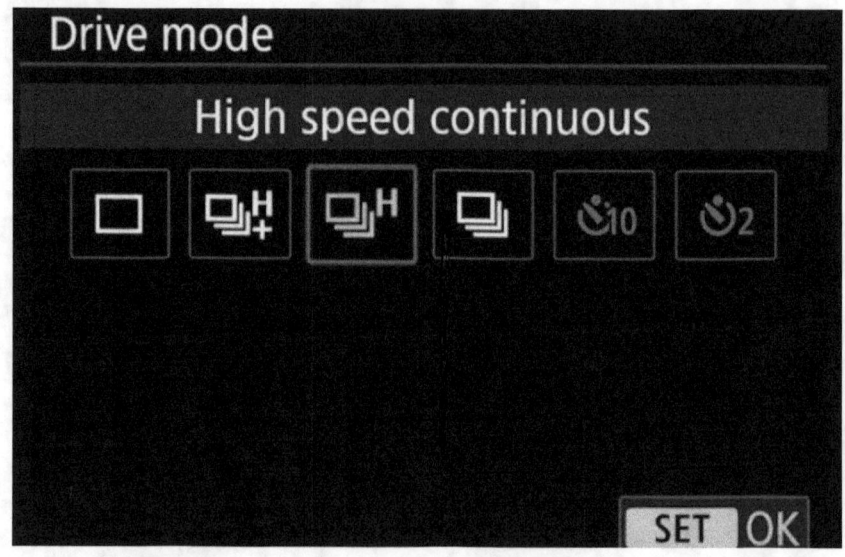

- **Mechanical:** You can take up to 6.5 shots in one second.
- **Electrical first curtain:** You can take up to 8 shots every second.
- **Electronic:** You can take up to 8 shots every second.

✓   Low-speed continuous shooting: You can take

continuous photos by pressing the shutter button all the way. It captures a maximum of 3.0 images per second when you keep the button pressed.

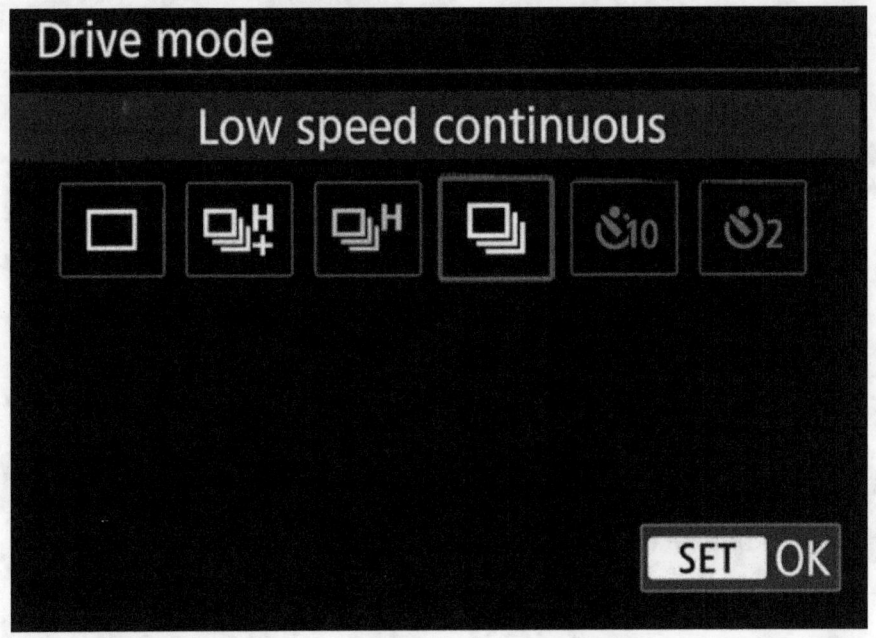

✓   Special fast and ongoing

✓   Wait for 10 seconds before each picture is taken using the 10-second self-timer.

✓   Wait for 2 seconds before each picture is taken using the self-timer.

Use the Self-Timer

Use the self-timer when you want to be in a group photo. Just press the DRIVE-AF button on your camera for 6 seconds while you're looking at the screen

Turn the Quick Control dial 2 to select one.

√ 10-sec Self-timer: Snap a picture in 10 seconds

√ 2-sec Self-timer: Take a picture in 2 seconds

Choose how many pictures you want to take in a row (between 2 and 10) in the Shooting menu or quick control screen.

- **Focus:** Do this by pressing the shutter button halfway
- **Take the picture:** Pressing it all the way.

Look at the blinking light and listen for the quick beeps. Then, check the seconds on the screen to make sure it's working. The light blinks fast, and the camera beeps rapidly for about two seconds before taking a picture.

CHAPTER 3: MASTERING COLOR CONTROLS

Understanding the White Balance Setting

In photography, white balance is adjusted to balance the color of the light source so that a white object looks white. You can use different light sources such as sunlight, incandescent bulbs, and fluorescent lights to illuminate different objects. In the literal sense, these different light sources may look colorless, but in reality, they emit different colors. Digital camera image effects reproduce these color differences as they are, so your photos may look different depending on the light source, without any other color adjustments.

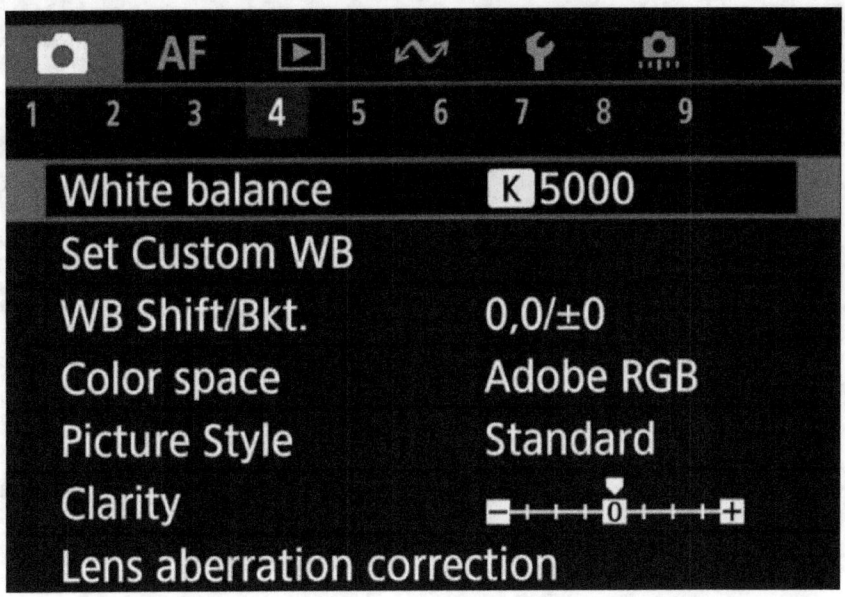

Automatic white balance fixes colors in photos without the photographer doing anything. It makes sure the picture looks right, like turning a photo taken in blue light to not look too red. If it doesn't work perfectly, the photographer can pick different options based on the lighting. They can even make the photo intentionally reddish or bluish for a specific effect.

Auto White Balance

Our eyes adjust to different lights, making white things look white in any light. Cameras use color temperature to figure out white and adjust pictures to look natural. With "Ambience Priority," photos get a bit warmer in incandescent light. "White Priority" makes warm colors less intense in the picture.

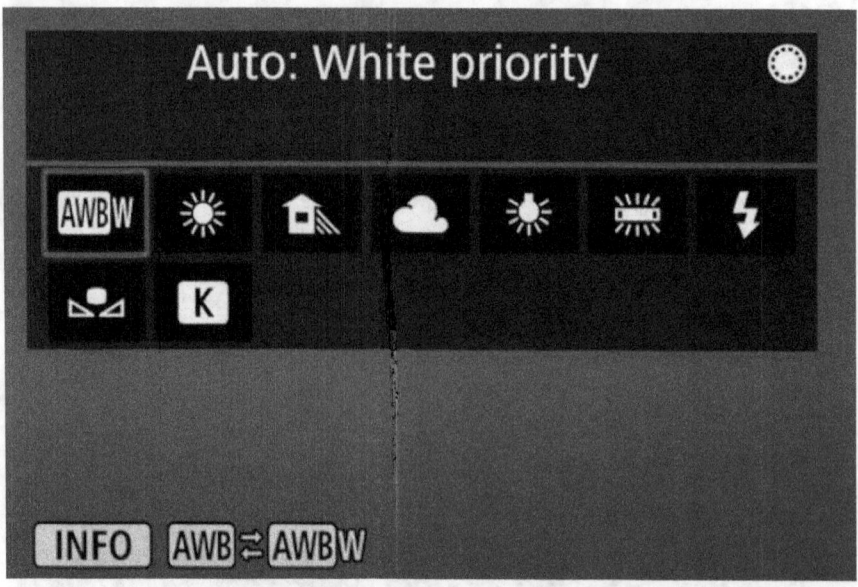

To access your camera settings, press the MENU button. Turn the Quick control dial 2 to pick the Shooting menu tab. Use the

Main dial to select shooting tab 4. Turn Quick control dial 1 to choose White Balance, then press the SET button.

Turn the Quick control dial to select AWB, then press the INFO icon.

Turn the Quick control dial 1 to pick either option /. Press the SET icon to confirm the changes.

Color Temperature

You can pick a number to choose how warm or cool the colors look in your photo.

To access your camera settings, press the MENU button. Turn the Quick control dial 2 to pick the Shooting menu. Use the Main dial to select shooting tab 4. Turn the Quick control dial 1 to choose White Balance, then press SET.

Turn the Quick control dial 1 to pick. Turn the Main dial to change the color temperature, then press the SET button. You can choose color temperatures from 2500K to 10000K in increments of 100K.

White Balance Adjustment

Once you've chosen the right white balance, you can tweak it. Think of this tweak like using filters to change color temperature, which you can buy in stores.

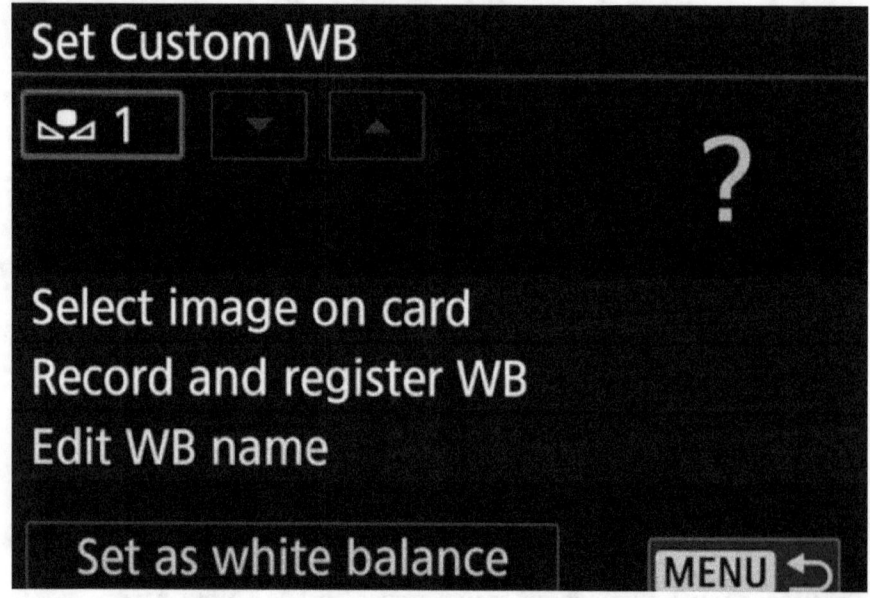

There are 2 color temperature adjustments available for you to make:

- White balance correction
- White Balance Bracketing

White balance correction

To access your camera settings, press the MENU button. Turn the Quick control dial 2 to pick the Shooting menu. Use the Main dial to select shooting tab 4. Turn Quick control dial 1 to choose WB Shift/Bkt, and press the SET button.

Move the small mark on the screen where you want by rolling the Multi-controller along the AGBM axes.

B is Blue, A is Amber, M is Magenta, and G is Green. To fix the colors, move the mark in the direction you want the white balance to go.

Look at the top left of the screen to see which way and how much you need to correct (like A2 or G1). Press Erase to undo all White Balance Shift and Bracket settings. Press SET to finish and leave the settings.

White Balance Bracketing

With White Balance Bracketing, you can quickly capture a scene in three photos, each with a different color tone for the white balance.

Adjusting the amount of white balance bracketing

Press the MENU button on your camera to open the menus. Turn the Quick control dial 2 to pick the Shooting menu tab. Use the Main dial to select shooting tab 4. Turn Quick control dial 1 to choose WB Shift/Bkt, and press the SET button.

Turn the Quick control dial to change the mark on the screen from 1 to 3. Turning it right adjusts the B/A bracketing, and turning it left adjusts the M/G bracketing.

The top left corner shows the direction and amount of bracketing (like 0, 0/BA±3). If you press the Erase button, it cancels all WB Shift/B&W settings. To exit the settings, click the SET button.

Taking a Quick Look at Picture Styles

By choosing a Picture Style, you can make your digital photos look the way you want. It's like how photographers used different films in the past to get a specific look for their pictures.

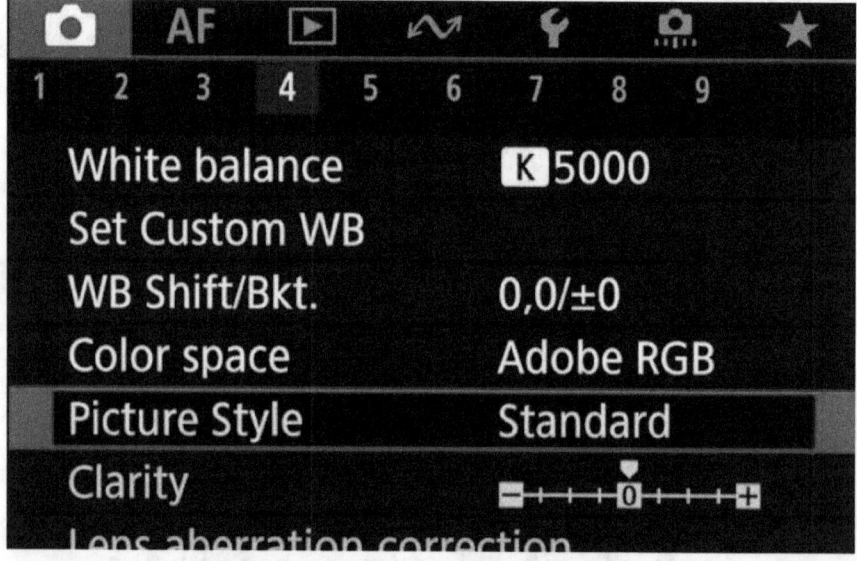

Canon's Picture Styles offer different ways to manage your images, like Standard, Auto, Portrait, Landscape, Fine, Neutral, Faithful, Monochrome, etc. They help you easily tweak different settings for your pictures.

How to Select a Picture Style

To access your camera settings, press the MENU button. Use the Quick Control dial 2 to pick the Shooting menu tab. Turn the Main dial to select shooting tab 4. Twist Quick control dial

1 to highlight Picture Style, then press SET. Choose a picture style by turning the Quick control dial 1 and pressing SET.

Picture Style	(S,(F,(T,0,&,0
[A] Auto	4,2,3,0,0,0
[S] Standard	4,2,3,0,0,0
[P] Portrait	3,2,4,0,0,0
[L] Landscape	5,2,3,0,0,0
[FD] Fine Detail	4,1,1,0,0,0
[N] Neutral	0,2,2,0,0,0
INFO Detail set.	SET OK

Choose how you want your pictures to look:

a) **Auto:** Adjusts colors based on surroundings, making them vibrant.

b) **Standard:** Makes images vivid, crisp, and sharp—good for most scenes.

c) **Portrait:** Creates even skin tones with less sharpness, ideal for close-up portraits. Adjust skin tones as needed.

d) **Landscape:** Enhances blues and greens for sharp and vibrant images, great for landscapes.

e) **Fine Detail (FD):** Shows all the small details of your subject with slightly lighter colors.

f) **Neutral (N):** Good if you want to edit your image on a computer later. It makes the image smaller and less contrasting for a natural look.

g) **Faithful:** Also great for computer editing. It keeps the original colors measured under sunlight. Reduce contrast for a calmer image.

h) **Monochrome:** Turns your image into black and white.

i) **User Defined 1–3:** You can create your styles based on presets like [Portrait] and [Landscape], adjusting them as needed. Unregistered styles use default settings.

Picture Style icons

The pictures on the Style selection screen show things like Strength, Fineness, Threshold, Contrast, Sharpness, and more. The numbers tell you the specific settings for each of these things in the chosen image style.

Sharpness means how clear the image is. Strength is how powerful something appears. Fineness is about the level of detail. The threshold is the point where something starts to happen. Contrast is the difference between light and dark. Saturation is the intensity of colors. The color tone is the overall color feel. The filter effect in monochrome is a black-and-white filter. The tone effect in monochrome is a black-and-white tone adjustment.

How to Customize Your Picture Style

You can make each picture style your own by adjusting the starting settings.

Push MENU, use the Quick Control Dial 2 to pick the Shooting menu, turn the Main dial to select Shooting tab 4, use Quick Control Dial 1 to choose Picture Style, and press SET.

Turn the Quick control dial 1 to choose a picture style.

Now, press the INFO button.

Turn the Quick control dial to pick an option, then push the SET button.

Change the effect level, and press SET. Save changes by pressing MENU and go back to Picture Style. Altered settings are shown in blue.

CHAPTER 4: CHOOSING BASIC PICTURE SETTINGS

Resolution and File Type (The Image Quality Setting)

Quality

Image and Video Quality

Fantastic image quality even at high ISOs, impressive color balance, and excellent video capabilities with 4K/60p and oversampled 6K/60p. If you already own an EOS R5 or R6 and want better image quality, the EOS R3 with its 24-megapixel sensor may not be a significant upgrade, especially if you're hoping for a revolution in low-light performance and dynamic range.

The pictures from the Canon EOS R3 are great, not bad at all. The camera is excellent at capturing pleasing images, especially in low light, thanks to its top-notch color processing. It's even better than the EOS R5 in high ISO, going up to 102,400.

Our tests showed that ISO settings up to 1600 look the same. If you go up to ISO 3200, you might see a bit of noise in less detailed areas. Continuing to ISO 12,800 gives a film-like grain, but noticeable cloudy noise only starts at ISO 51,200.

The R3 camera takes great photos, especially for press, astrophotography, sports in different weather, and weddings.

It's reliable and works well even at ISO settings that were once unthinkable.

Before Canon officially introduced the EOS R3, they didn't talk much about the camera's video features. However, it's important to note that these features are significant. The camera is powerful and can shoot high-quality videos, including raw video at 6K/60p and oversampled 4K/60p footage. This is not common for cameras like this one.

When a video is oversampled, it usually has more details and less noise, which is good. The new stacked sensor in the EOS R3 effectively reduces the rolling shutter in video mode, especially noticeable when the camera moves quickly.

When you record videos in super high quality (6K raw), you can use the Cinema Raw Light format to make the file sizes smaller without losing the dynamic range. Filmmakers will like that it supports C-Log 3 for better color grading. The EOS R3 also handles overheating better than the EOS R5 did before updates.

The R3's bigger body and lower-resolution sensor help spread its parts more, letting you shoot for about six hours at regular speed or one and a half hours at high speed, as long as your camera has enough power.

The EOS R3's video capabilities get a boost from the new Multi-Function Shoe. It can charge attachments like the new Directional Stereo Microphone DM-E1D. Plus, you can record video to both the CFexpress and UHS-II slots at the same time for a backup.

JPEG/HEIFF Image Quality

To make JPEG and HEIF images from RAW photos, follow these steps to adjust the image quality:

1. Press the MENU button to open your camera settings. Turn the Quick control dial 2 to pick the Shooting menu. Use the Main dial to select shooting tab 1. Turn Quick control dial 1 to choose JPEG/HEIF quality, and press the SET button.

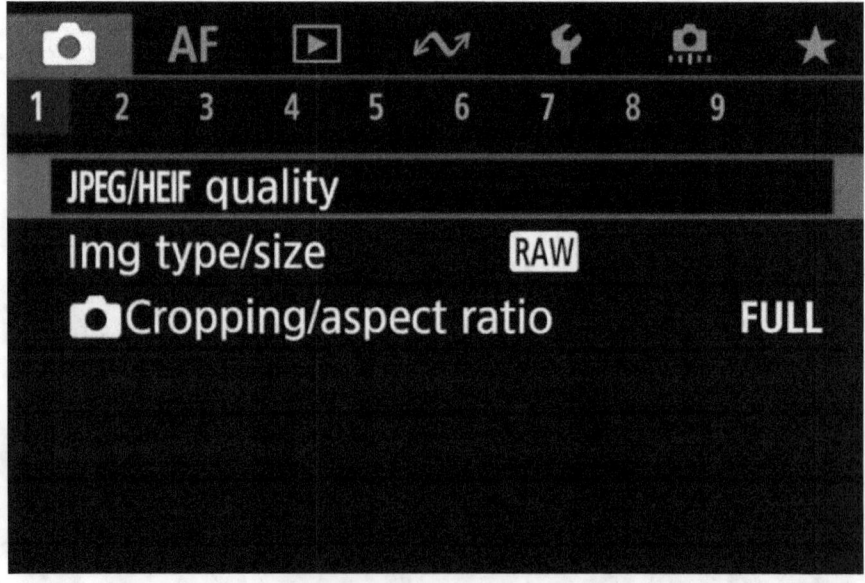

2. Pick a picture size (Large, Medium, Small1, or Small2) and push the SET button.
3. Set the desired quality (compression).
4. Choose a number from 1 to 10 and click SET. A higher number means better quality, with 6 to 10 being good and 1 to 5 marked as lower quality.

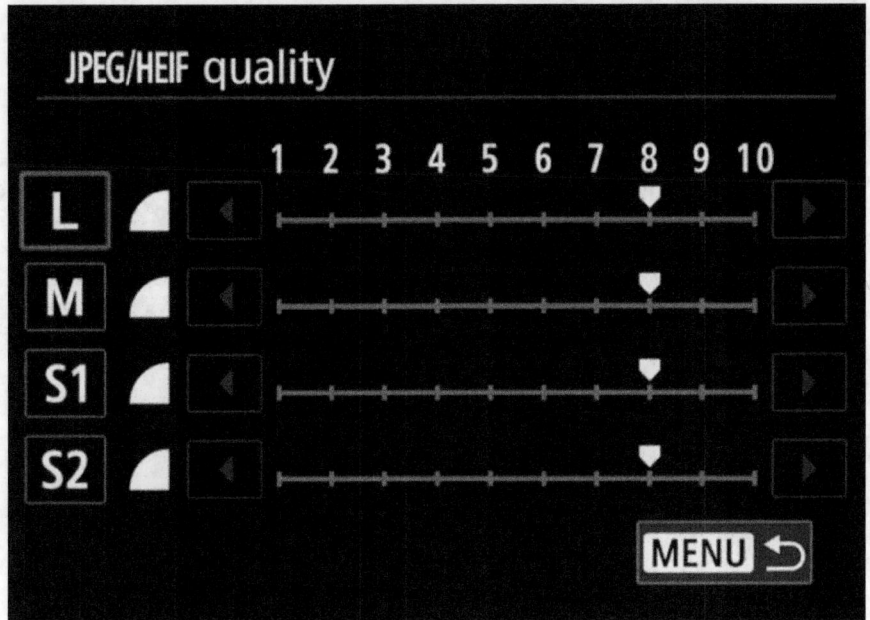

Cropping/Aspect Ratio

When you use RF or EF lenses, pictures are usually taken on a sensor about 36.0 x 24.0mm in full-frame mode. If you switch to a cropped mode, it's like zooming in (similar to a telephoto lens) and enlarging the center part by about 1.6 times (APS-C size). With an EF-S lens, it captures a 3:2 area in the center and magnifies it by about 1.6x (APS-C size).

To adjust the shape or cut the picture, follow these steps:

1. Press the MENU button on your camera, use the Quick Control Dial 2 to pick the Shooting menu, turn the Main dial to select Shooting Tab 1, use Quick Control Dial 1 to choose Cropping/aspect ratio, and press the SET button.

2. Turn the Quick control dial to pick an option. The chosen setting will be shown in blue. You can choose from Full Frame, 1.6x (cropped), 1:1, 4:3, or 16:9. If you're using EF-S lenses, it will automatically be set to 1.6x (cropped) with no other choices.

3. To keep the photo frame unchanged, tap the SET icon and take your picture. Choose how the photo frame looks. Click INFO, pick a display style (masked or outlined), and tap SET. Snap a photo. If you set [1.6x (crop)] or use an EF-S lens, the image is 1.6 times bigger. With [1:1], [4:3], or [16:9], the picture fits inside a black mask or outline.

Considering resolution: Large, Medium, or Small?

Choose between JPEG, HEIF, or RAW for your image quality. For JPEG and HEIF, pick from sizes L, M, S1, or S2. For RAW images, select either RAW or CRAW. Follow these steps to set your image size:

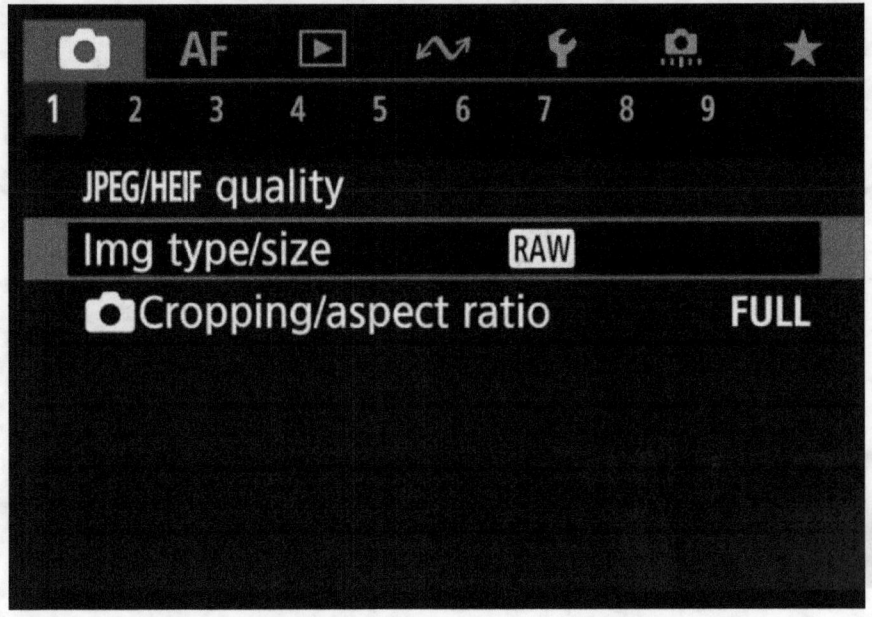

Choose Img type/size:

Press MENU, use the dials to navigate to the camera settings, choose the shooting options, and adjust image size based on your preference, whether you're recording separately or using standard settings.

a. **Standard (or Record to multiple)**
Turn the Main dial to pick the size for RAW images, or turn Quick control dial 1 for JPEG/HEIF images. Press the SET button to apply your changes.

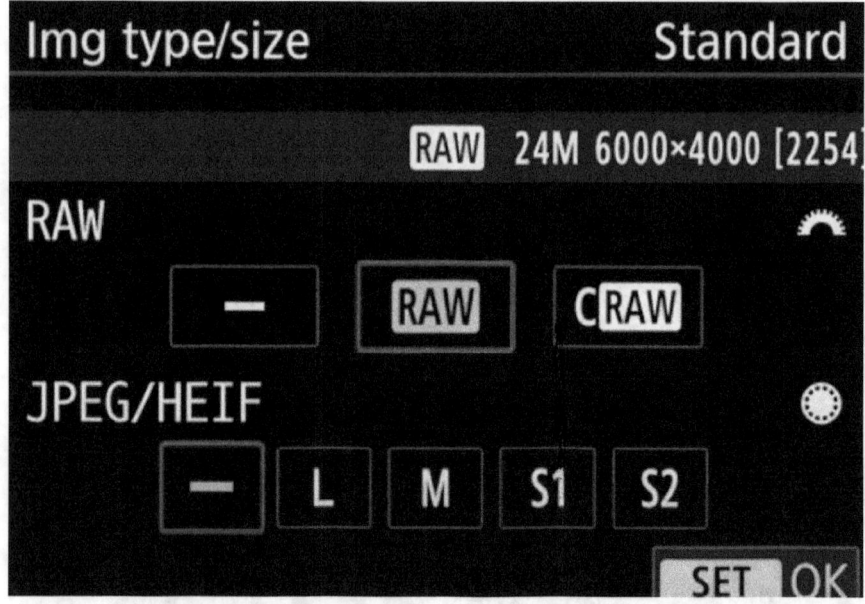

b. Record separately

If you want to record separately on either card 1 or card 2, turn the Quick control dial to choose the card and press the SET button. Also, remember that RAW images can be recorded as RAW or CRAW and can be saved independently. Pick an image size on the screen, then click SET.

Understanding file type (JPEG or RAW)

RAW Image

A RAW image is the untouched data from the camera sensor, stored as RAW or CRAW. CRAW makes smaller RAW files. You can edit RAW images and save them as JPEG or HEIF. In the Playback menu, go to Tab 2 and select 'RAW image processing.'

The original RAW image stays the same, letting you create various JPEG or HEIF versions.

You can edit RAW photos with Digital Photo Professional, an EOS software. Adjust the images as needed and save them in formats like JPEG or HEIF to keep the changes you make.

Image Processing

A RAW image is like the unprocessed data captured by your camera. It can be saved as RAW or CRAW. Your camera can then turn these into regular JPEG or HEIF images. Since RAW keeps the original data, you can adjust how it's processed and make multiple JPEG images.

You can edit RAW photos with software like Digital Photo Professional. For regular images (JPEG or HEIF), you can resize them, crop them, and convert them between formats like JPEG and HEIF. This chapter will show you how to do these things.

RAW Image Processing

Press MENU to open your camera settings. Turn the Quick Control dial 2 to select the Playback menu. Choose Playback tab 2. Turn the Quick control dial 1 to pick RAW image processing, then press SET.

Turn the Quick control dial to pick either "Select images" or "Select range," and then press the SET button.

If you pick "Select images," turn the Quick control dial to choose the image, then press the SET button. After that, press the Quick control button.

Pick a starting image, pick an ending image, and all the pictures in between will be marked. Do this for each set of images. Press the MENU button and set the processing conditions.

When you take pictures, the way they look will be based on the settings you used when taking them. If you turn on HDR while taking the pictures, they will be saved in a format called HEIF. If HDR is off, they will be saved as JPEG.

Choose Setup processing, First, pick between JPEG or Setup processing and then HEIF. Use the Multi-controller to select an item. Turn the quick control dial or main dial to change the options and press SET. To reset all settings, press the AE lock button and choose OK when you see the verification message.

You can adjust these things in RAW images using icons:

- Brightness
- White balance
- Picture Style
- Clarity
- Auto Lighting Optimizer
- High ISO speed Noise Reduction
- Image quality
- Color space sRGB
- Lens aberration correction

Turn Quick Control Dial 2 and Quick Control Dial 1 to switch between the screens for After Change and Shot Settings. The orange items on the After Change screen have been modified after the photo was taken. Press the MENU button to go back to the processing conditions screen.

After picking JPEG or HEIF, click the Save icon on the Setup processing screen. Read the message, and click OK. If you want to do this for more images, click Yes and do the same steps again.

Pick either the original or processed image, and then see the chosen image on the screen.

Render images with a specified aspect ratio

You can change RAW photos taken in square, standard, or widescreen shapes to regular pictures in the same shape, like JPEG or HEIF.

RAW image processing options

You can change these settings when working with RAW images. Check the specific chapters for more details on each setting.

1. Adjust how bright or dark your picture is, going up or down in small steps.
2. Pick how colors look in your photo. You can choose Auto: Focus on the surroundings or Auto: Focus on white.
3. Choose the style of your photo and tweak things like sharpness and contrast.

4. Make your picture clearer or softer on a scale from -4 to +4, but not in HEIF quality.
5. Set up automatic improvement for your photo's exposure. It helps fix pictures taken in weird lighting or with flash. Face exposure doesn't work with HEIF images.
6. Reduce grainy look in low-light photos
7. Make photos taken in low light look smoother by adjusting the noise reduction setting at high ISO values. To see the effect better, zoom in on the picture.
8. Choose how clear you want your photos
9. Decide the quality of your pictures when saving them as JPEG or HEIF images.
10. Pick your color style: sRGB or Adobe RGB
11. Choose between sRGB or Adobe RGB for color representation. If you're viewing on a camera monitor, Adobe RGB won't make a big difference. When using HEIF, HDR PQ is displayed but cannot be selected.
12. Fix lens issues
13. Correct various lens problems, like dark corners in photos. Enable peripheral illumination correction to fix dark corners, and zoom in to check the results. If it's still hard to see, use Digital Photo Professional for further correction.

This helps fix image distortion caused by the lens. When turned on, it shows the corrected image, which trims the edges. The image resolution might seem a bit lower, so you can tweak sharpness using the Picture Style's Sharpness setting if needed.

Fix blurriness, color issues, and filter loss in photos by adjusting the optical settings. Try the "High" or "Normal" options to see the changes when zoomed in. If the picture isn't enlarged, the "High" setting won't take effect. Choosing "High" or "Standard" corrects both color and dispersion problems, even though there are no visible options for these corrections.

The lens can cause colored fringes around the subject, known as chromatic aberration. You can fix this by turning on the [Enable] option, and the corrected image will be shown. If it's difficult to notice the changes, try zooming in on the image.

This helps fix blurriness caused by aperture changes. If you turn it on, the patch image will be turned off.

Resize JPEG/HEIF images

You can make a JPEG or HEIF picture smaller by reducing its pixels and saving it as a new one. You can resize L, M, or S1 JPEGs and all HEIF sizes except S2, including RAW+JPEG and RAW+HEIF images. But you can't resize S2 pictures, RAW images, or videos.

Press MENU to open your camera settings. Turn the Quick Control dial 2 to select the Playback menu. Choose Playback tab 2. Turn the Quick control dial 1 to pick Resize, then press the SET button.

Turn the Quick control dial to pick a picture, then press the SET button. You can also choose an image by tapping it on the index screen (if you're in index view).

Turn the Main dial or Quick control dial 2 to pick a size for your picture, then press the SET button.

To save, select OK for your resized image. Make sure to check the folder and file number, then choose [OK]. Repeat these steps for another image.

Cropping HEIF/JPEG

You can cut down JPEG and HEIF images from HDR photos, but you can't trim 4K videos or RAW images.

Press the MENU button to open your camera menus. Turn the Quick Control dial 2 to select the Playback menu tab. Choose tab 3 for Playback. Turn the Quick control dial 1 to pick Cropping, then press the SET button.

Turn the Quick control dial to pick a picture, and press the SET button. If you're in index view, you can also choose an image by touching the screen.

Press the SET button to open the cropping frame.

Your camera will cut off parts of the picture inside the frame.

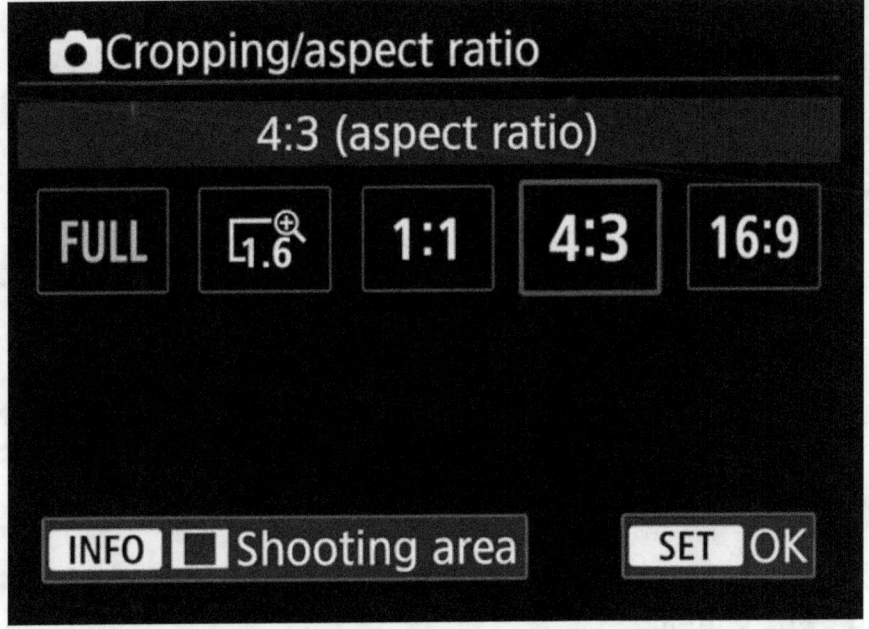

Turn the Main dial to change the frame size.

For tilting the frame, turn Quick control dial 1, select the icon, and press SET. Then, rotate the Quick control dial. After adjusting, press SET.

To change the frame's aspect ratio, turn Quick control dial 1, choose the icon and press SET. Use the Multi-controller to move the frame.

To preview the cropped area, turn Quick control dial 1, select the icon, and press SET. The camera will display the cropped image area.

Turn the Quick control dial to pick the Save icon, then press the SET button. Pick OK. Check the folder and file number, and choose [OK]. Do these steps again for another image resize.

Convert HEIF image to JPEG

You can change fancy HDR photos (HEIF format) into regular JPEG pictures.

Press the MENU button to open your camera menus. Turn the Quick Control dial 2 to select the Playback menu. Go to Playback tab 2. Turn the Quick control dial 1 to pick HEIF to JPEG conversion, then press the SET button.

Rotate the Quick control dial 1 to choose Select Images. Push the SET button.

Turn the dial to pick a photo, and press SET. To choose a pic from the index screen, touch it. Repeat for more photos. Press the Quick Control button.

Select OK for the new image. Click Yes if there are more images to convert.

Turn the dial to pick Original or Processed. Press SET. Original shows the HEIF image, and Processed shows the converted JPEG.

Specify a Group/Range of images you want converted

View your pictures in the index display.

Press the MENU button to open your camera menus. Turn the Quick Control dial 2 to select the Playback menu. Choose Playback tab 2. Turn the Quick control dial 1 to pick HEIF to JPEG conversion, and press the SET button.

Turn the Quick control dial to pick "Select range," and press the SET button.

Indicate the range of pictures to protect:

Pick the last image. The range between them gets marked with a check. Do this again for more images.

Press the "Quick control" button.

Select OK to save the new JPEG image.

If you have more images, click Yes to convert them.

Rotate the Quick control dial 1 to pick either the Original image or the Processed image. Push the SET button.

If you choose the Original image, the original HEIF image will be displayed. But if you picked the Processed image, the JPEG image you converted will be displayed.

Adding Flash

Use the flash

To use the flash easily, just connect it to the top of your camera using the hot shoe. For now, that's all you need to do. Note:

Speedlights and flashes are the same, and Speedlite is just what Canon calls their flashes.

If you have a Sony camera, it's called a Multi Interface Shoe, and for Nikon, it's an Accessory Shoe.

Later on, when you're comfortable with using the flash, you can explore using it off-camera (remote flash photography). But for now, don't complicate things. Focus on connecting the flash to your camera. Take it step by step, and you'll get the hang of it. No need to rush!

Connect the flash to the camera

Attach the flash to the camera using the hot shoe. Before inserting, make sure the flash isn't locked, and gently slide it in. Don't apply too much force to avoid damaging the contacts. If it doesn't fit easily, check if the flash lock is open. Push the flash forward and use the locking dial to secure it in place to prevent potential damage.

Activate Flash Photography

First, turn on the flash. Go to your camera menus by pressing the MENU button. Use the dials to navigate: Quick Control dial 2 for the Shooting menu, Main dial for tab 3. Now, choose External Speedlite control and press SET.

Next, pick Flash firing by rotating Quick control dial 1 and pressing SET. Choose Enable and press SET again to activate the flash for photography. If you choose Disable, the flash won't fire, but the AF assist beam will still work.

Flash Settings

Ready to use your camera flash? Before we dive in, let's take a step back. Check the flash settings first. There are many options, but we'll focus on the basic ones for now. Adjust these settings from your camera's menu screen after attaching and turning on the flash in the hot shoe. Stick to the simple settings until you're comfortable moving on to more advanced ones.

Ensure to take these steps to change the flash settings:

1. Choose External Speedlight control: Press MENU, use the dials to select shooting settings and choose External Flash control. Then, go to Flash Function Settings, select your desired settings, and press SET.
2. On the next screen, you'll see these icons:
   - Flash mode
   - Wireless functions / Firing ratio control (RATIO)
   - Flash zoom (flash coverage)
   - Shutter synchronization
   - Flash exposure compensation
   - Flash exposure bracketing
3. Turn the Quick control dial to select an icon, then press the SET button.

Flash mode

After selecting Flash Function Settings, turn the main dial to pick a flash mode, then press the SET button. If your Speedlight has a mode button, use that to choose the flash mode. Refer to your Speedlight's manual if you're unsure where the mode button is.

We'll look at these flash modes for the Canon EOS R3:

1. Manual (M) flash mode
2. Multi flash mode
3. TTL (or ETTL) flash mode

There are also other flash modes:

- CSP (Continuous shooting priority)
- Ext. A
- Ext. M

Manual flash mode

This setting is the simplest to handle, but you have to manage the light yourself. It's not recommended for beginners. If you're getting unpredictable results with manual mode and flash, hold off until you're more familiar with using the flash. It can be challenging, and even experts can slip up, so don't be discouraged.

Multi Flash Mode

It has also an advanced mode. This flash mode is used to create images where the flash fires multiple times during a single camera exposure, creating the effect of motion.

Let's ignore that too for now. You may never actually use it. Many professional photographers we've met have never had the chance to use this.

TTL/ETTL flash mode

TTL, or "Through The Lens," is a mode where the camera's flash first sends out a quick invisible flash. Then, the camera figures out how far the subject is and how much light is needed. After that, it adjusts the flash power to give the right amount of light for a good picture. It's a good setting to use, especially if you're just starting with flash photography. When you set up your camera well (we'll cover that too), TTL and your camera work together smoothly.

Flash Exposure Compensation

Make sure your camera flash is set up properly. There's one more thing to understand: Flash Exposure Compensation (FEC). It lets you adjust how much light your flash adds to your photos. Usually, it's fine to keep it at zero. You can change it using a button and dial on your flash – look for a lightning bolt with a +/- sign. If your camera and flash are from the same brand, you might also adjust FEC in the camera menu.

Follow these steps to enable you to set the Flash exposure compensation from the camera:

- To access your camera settings, press the MENU button. Turn the quick control dial to pick the Shooting menu. Use the Main dial to select shooting tab 3. Turn the Quick control dial to choose External Speedlight (or Speedlite) control, and press the SET button.
- Turn the Quick control dial to pick Flash Function Settings, then press SET. Choose the flash exposure compensation icon by turning the dial and pressing SET. If you set it to negative, the flash is dimmer; if positive, it's brighter.

85

Camera Flash Exposure settings

This part talks about the main camera settings for beginners. There are four common exposure modes: Program Auto, Aperture Priority, Shutter Priority, and Manual.

Canon EOS cameras have five main shooting modes, shown by the symbols Fv, P, Tv, Av, M, and Bulb. Here's a quick breakdown:

- Fv is Flexible-Priority AE.
- P is like Program Auto Mode.
- Tv is Shutter-Priority AE, similar to Aperture Priority Mode.
- Av is Aperture-Priority AE, also similar to Aperture Priority Mode.
- M is Manual Mode.
- BULB is for long exposures.

Your camera has different shooting modes like AUTO, User modes, and Custom modes. To choose a shooting mode, use the MODE button and other buttons like the Main dial. Avoid using Manual mode with TTL flash for simplicity. Let the camera and flash handle it. Use different shooting settings based on the situation.

Program Mode

If you're new to photography and unsure about exposure and settings, just use Program mode. It's okay, and it often captures nice pictures.

I often use this camera setup without a tripod for various situations. However, when using the flash indoors, there are some issues to watch out for. If you choose a small aperture like f/8 or f/11, you'll need to set the flash to a higher power, which can drain the battery or make the flash overheat.

This might result in a dark background, slow shutter speed (especially in low light), a ghostly subject, and a blurry picture. So, be cautious when using this setting. Keep your camera aperture wide open, and using a lens with a large aperture, like a 50mm f/1.8, can be helpful.

Shutter Priority Mode

To avoid issues, use a shutter speed below your camera's recommended sync speed. Imagine taking a photo and seeing a black bar because the shutter closes before the flash finishes.

If your camera's sync speed is 1/200 or 1/250, don't go faster. Even a slower speed like 1/30 works well, as the flash freezes the moment. Check your camera's manual or search online for its sync speed to prevent problems.

Try This Activity:

Take pictures in dark places or rooms with low light using these settings:

- Choose Shutter priority for Camera exposure mode.
- Use ETTL for Flash mode and set FEC to zero.
- Set the Shutter speed to 1/30s.
- Use Auto range for ISO (set max to 3200 or 6400) or up to 800.

Just click the shutter, and the camera does the rest. If there's too much movement or the image is blurry, change the shutter speed to 1/60 or 1/100. If the background is too dark, increase the ISO.

Now, practice using Flash for an advantage in Flash Photography. Attach your flash to the camera, and capture great photos at your next event.

CHAPTER 5: TAKING CHARGE OF EXPOSURE

Introducing the Exposure

Shutter speed

Minimum Shutter Speed

You can make sure your camera doesn't use a very slow shutter speed automatically by setting a minimum shutter speed for ISO Auto. This helps when using different lenses or shooting modes, especially when capturing moving subjects. It also helps to avoid blurry shots caused by camera shake.

Here's how to set the minimum shutter speed:

1. Push the MENU button on your camera to open the menus. Turn the Quick control dial 2 to pick the Shooting menu tab. Use the Main dial to select shooting tab 2. Turn Quick control dial 1 to choose ISO speed settings, then press the SET button.
2. Turn the Quick control dial to pick Min. shutter speed, and press the SET button.
3. Turn the Quick control dial 1 to pick between Auto or Manual mode.
   - **For Auto:** If you pick Auto, turn the Main dial to make the speed either slower or faster than usual, and then tap SET.
   - **For Manual:** If you choose Manual, turn the Main dial to pick the shutter speed, and then press SET.

89

ISO Speed

ISO, also known as ISO speed or film speed, is a measure of a camera's sensitivity to light. It represents how strongly the camera's digital sensor or film responds to incoming light. A low ISO value indicates that the camera is less sensitive to light, requiring more light to capture a properly exposed image. Conversely, a high ISO value indicates greater sensitivity, allowing for sharper images in low-light conditions.

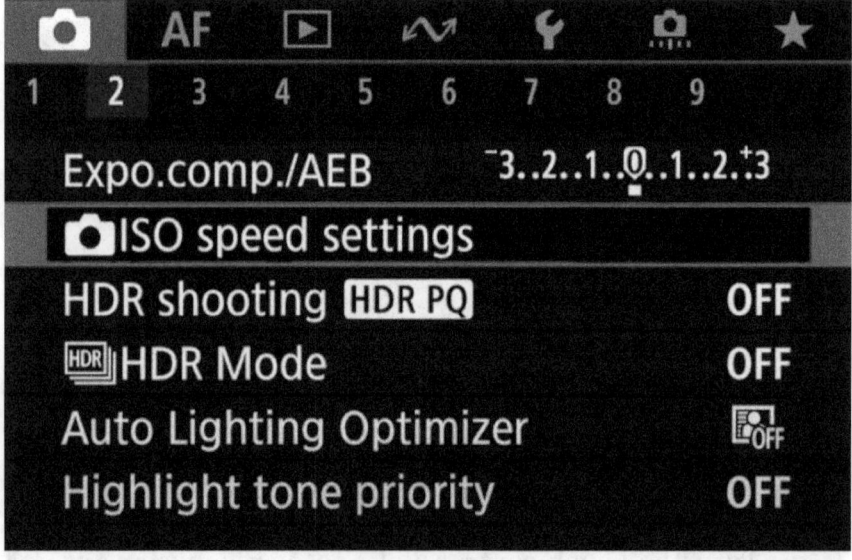

Adjusting the ISO setting is crucial for achieving optimal exposure in varying lighting conditions. In general, choosing a higher ISO value results in faster shutter speeds, enabling you to capture images with minimal blur, especially when shooting moving subjects. However, increasing the ISO also introduces digital noise, which appears as grainy or speckled patterns in the image.

In low-light environments, increasing the ISO allows you to capture images without excessively slow shutter speeds that would result in motion blur. By increasing the ISO, you enhance the sensitivity of the sensor, reducing the amount of light required for proper exposure at a given shutter speed. This, in turn, allows you to use faster shutter speeds to freeze motion and capture sharper images.

📷 ISO speed settings	
ISO speed	200
ISO speed range	100-102400
Auto range	100-25600
Min. shutter spd.	Auto
	MENU ↰

While higher ISO values can be beneficial in low-light situations, it's essential to balance image quality and ISO sensitivity. As the ISO value increases, so does the digital noise, which can compromise the overall image quality. Therefore, it's important to find the optimal ISO setting for each shooting situation, ensuring a balance between capturing a well-exposed image and minimizing noise.

Why is this so important?

Modern cameras are capable of producing high-quality images at significantly higher ISO settings compared to older cameras. This advancement allows you to capture images in dimly lit environments using faster shutter speeds, effectively minimizing camera shake and subject blur.

However, it's crucial to note that increasing the ISO also introduces digital noise, which manifests as grainy or speckled patterns in the image. While higher ISO values can be beneficial in low-light situations, it's essential to maintain a balance between image quality and ISO sensitivity. As the ISO value increases, so does the digital noise, which can compromise the overall image quality. Therefore, it's important to find the optimal ISO setting for each shooting situation, ensuring a balance between capturing a well-exposed image and minimizing noise.

To set the ISO speed on your camera, follow these steps:

1. Press the MENU button to access the camera's menus.
2. Rotate the Quick control dial 2 to select the Shooting menu tab.
3. Rotate the Main dial to choose shooting tab 2.
4. Rotate the Quick control dial 1 to select ISO speed settings, and then press the SET button.

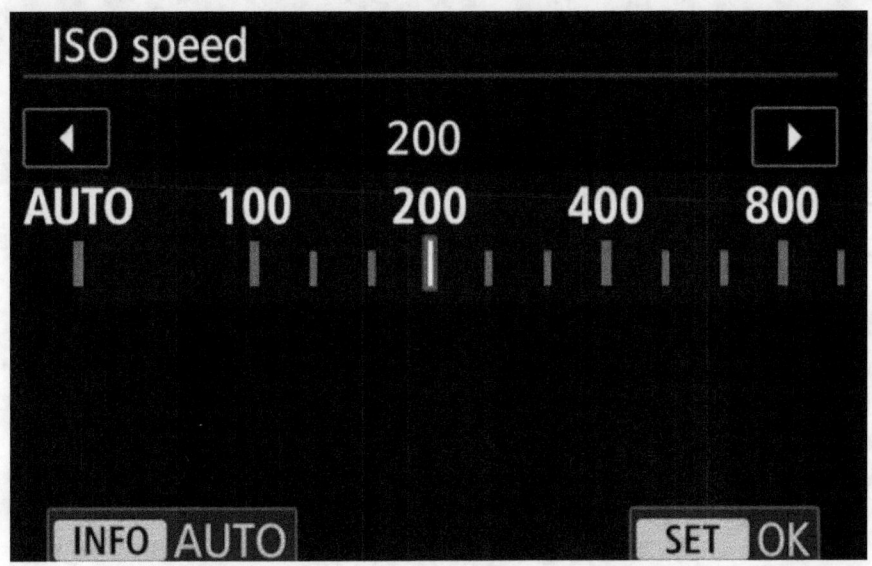

5. Rotate the Quick control dial 1 to choose the desired ISO speed, and then press the SET button.
6. Choose AUTO to automatically set the ISO. Choose Manual if you'll like to set the ISO yourself.
7. Press the MENU button to return to the shooting screen.
8. After closing the menu, the ISO mode you choose will be displayed on the bottom left side of the shooting screen.
9. To adjust the ISO speed in manual mode, while your image is showing on the screen, rotate the Quick control dial 2 to adjust the ISO speed. You can set ISO speeds from ISO 100 to 102400 in 1/3 step increments. If you choose Auto, you don't need to do anything.

Remember to find the optimal ISO setting for each shooting situation, ensuring a balance between capturing a well-exposed image and minimizing noise.

Tips for perfect ISO speed selection

Using lower ISO makes your photos less grainy, but it might make them blurry if there's not enough light or if there's movement.

Higher ISO helps in low light and expands the focused area, but it can make your photos noisier.

How to manually set the ISO Speed Range

You can choose the ISO setting range yourself. Set the low limit from L (like ISO 50) to ISO 102400, and the high limit from ISO 100 to H (like ISO 204800). Just follow these steps:

- **Select ISO speed settings:** Press MENU, use Quick Control Dial 2 for the Shooting menu, use Main dial for Shooting tab 2, use Quick Control Dial 1 to pick ISO speed, and press SET.
- **Choose ISO speed range:** Turn the Quick control dial 1 to pick the ISO speed range, and then press the SET button.
- **Set Minimum:** First, pick the Minimum box, then press the SET button. After that, select the ISO speed you prefer and press SET again.
- **Set Maximum:** Pick the box that says "Maximum" and press the SET button. Select the ISO speed you prefer, then press SET. Finally, choose OK.

ISO Speed Range for ISO Auto

You can choose the ISO sensitivity for automatic mode between 100 and 51200. You can set the lowest limit from 100 to 51200 and the highest limit from 200 to 51200 in step 1.

Press the MENU button on your camera to open the menus. Turn the Quick control dial 2 to pick the Shooting menu tab. Use the Main dial to select shooting tab 2. Turn Quick control dial 1 to choose ISO speed settings, and then press the SET button.

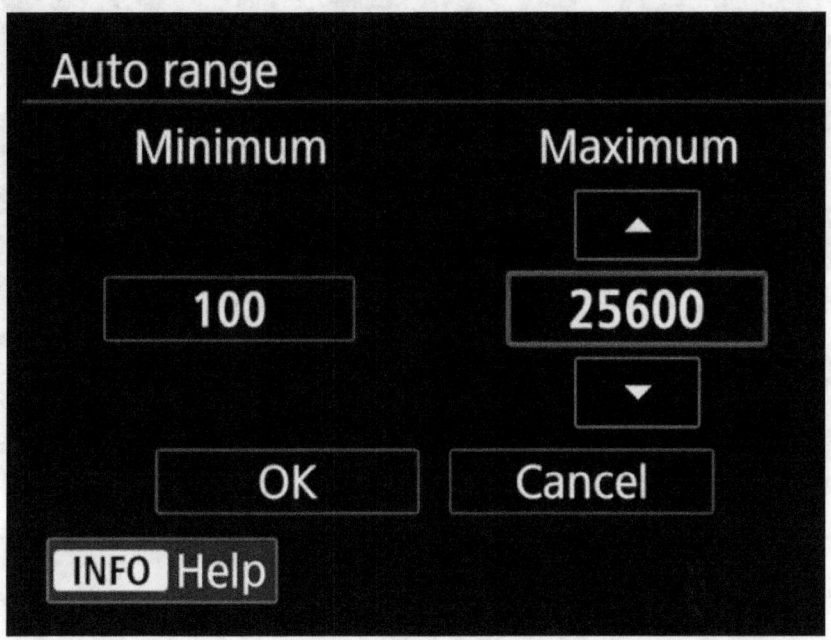

Turn the Quick control dial to select Auto range, and then press the SET button.

First, pick the Minimum box and press SET. Select the ISO speed you prefer, then press SET. Repeat these steps for the Maximum field.

Click OK.

Exposure Compensation

Exposure compensation can make your photo brighter or darker than the camera's usual setting.

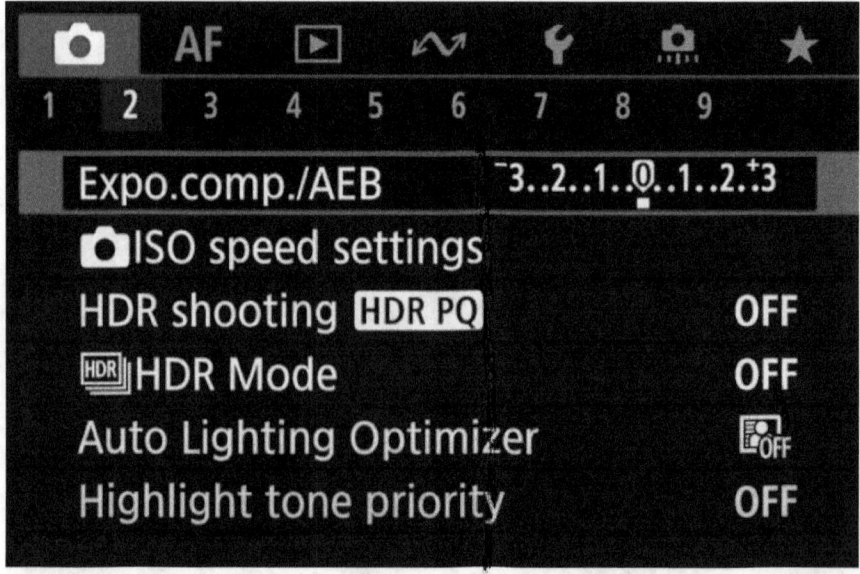

Manual Exposure Compensation

Adjust the brightness in FV, P, Tv, Av, and M modes by using exposure compensation. Here's how:

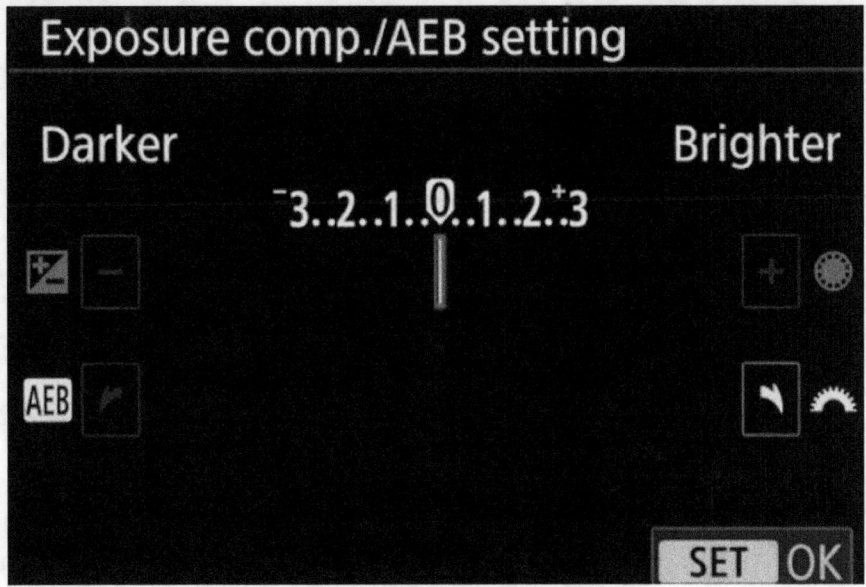

Hold the camera button halfway and look at the light level indicator.

Turn the Quick control dial to make your photo brighter or darker. Look at the screen while you do this. If you want a brighter picture, turn it one way; for a darker one, turn it the other way. A symbol on the screen will show the changes. Once you're done, take a photo. To go back to the normal exposure, set the exposure level bar to the standard index (arrow at the top).

Exposure compensation with ISO auto

When your camera's ISO is set to AUTO in manual mode, you can adjust exposure compensation like this:

1. Click the exposure level indicator.

2. Press MENU, go to the Shooting menu tab and scroll to Shooting tab 2.
3. Select item 2 (Expo.comp./AEB) and press SET.

To quickly access the control screen, press the Quick Control button. Adjust exposure by rotating the lens control ring while pressing the shutter button halfway.

AE lock

When you're taking pictures, use the exposure lock to set focus and brightness separately or when capturing several shots with the same brightness. Just press the AE lock button, adjust your shot, and snap a photo. AE lock works well when your subjects are lit from behind, like with sunlight or a window.

To ensure precise exposure in your photographs, utilize the AE Lock feature to maintain consistent exposure settings:

- Aim your camera at your subject and press the shutter button halfway. This will engage the camera's autofocus system and display the current exposure value.
- Once the desired focus and exposure are achieved, press the AE Lock button, typically labeled with an asterisk (*) or a lock symbol. This will lock the current exposure settings, preventing them from changing as you recompose your shot.
- With AE Lock engaged, you can now adjust the framing of your composition without affecting the exposure. Take your photo by fully pressing the shutter button.
- To capture multiple images while maintaining the locked exposure, simply press and hold the shutter button to take each subsequent shot. The AE Lock will

remain active until you release the shutter button or disable AE Lock by pressing the AE Lock button again.

CHAPTER 6: CAPTURING VIDEO

Videography With Canon EOS R3

Program AE Video Recording mode

In this mode, your camera adjusts the brightness for you based on the scene. To use it, switch to video mode, push the MODE dial, select (Program AE) on the screen by turning the main dial, and press the SET button.

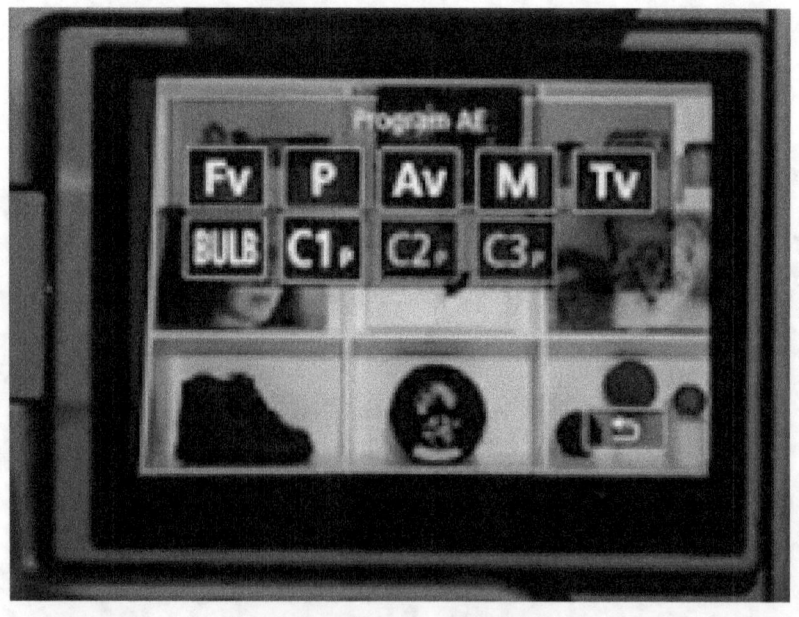

To focus on your subjects, press the shutter button halfway to focus on the chosen area. Before recording a video, you can use Auto-focus or Manual focus. Typically, Movie Servo AF is on, ensuring your camera stays focused on the subject.

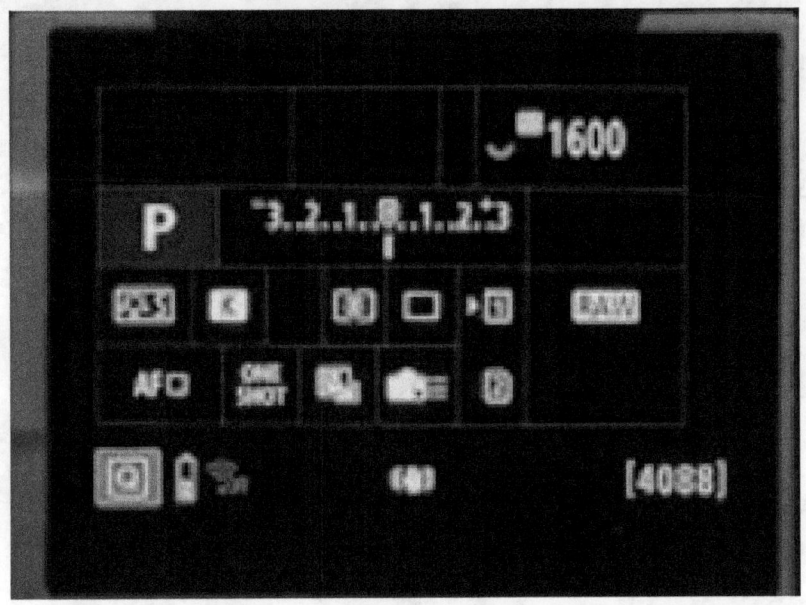

To begin recording your video, press the shutter button halfway to focus on the chosen area. Before recording a video, you can use Auto-focus or Manual focus. Typically, Movie Servo AF is on, ensuring your camera stays focused on the subject.

Shutter priority AE Video Recording

In video mode, choose Shutter priority. Adjust the shutter speed, and the camera will automatically set ISO and aperture for the right brightness. Switch to video mode, turn the MODE dial, pick Shutter-Priority AE on the screen, and press SET.

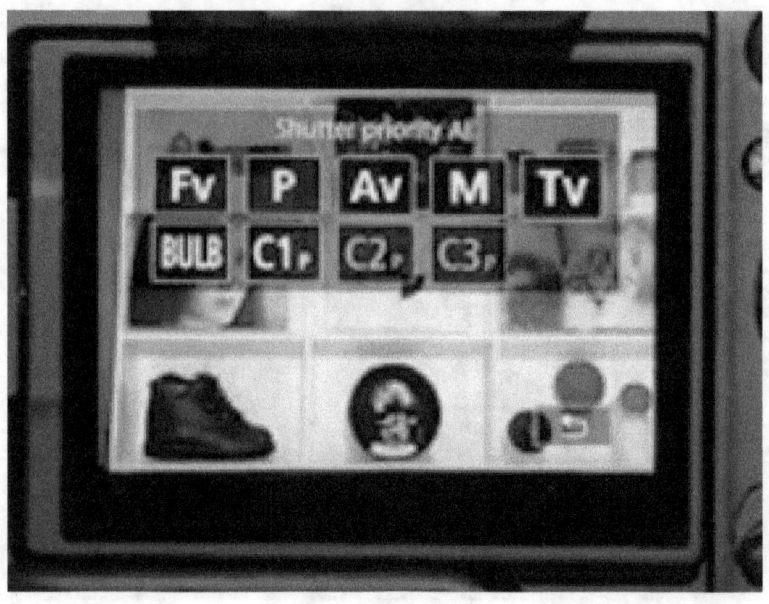

Adjust the shutter speed (1): Turn the big dial and check the screen to change how fast your camera takes pictures. The speed options depend on how quickly the camera captures each frame.

Focus on your subjects: Press the shutter button halfway to focus on the chosen area. You can use Auto-focus or Manual focus before recording a video. Typically, Movie Servo AF is on, ensuring your camera stays focused on the subject.

Begin recording your video: Press the movie shooting button to start recording. You can also begin recording by tapping the red dot on the screen. While recording, you'll see the REC icon at the top right, and the camera's microphone will capture sound. Stop recording by pressing the movie shooting button or clicking the red square on the screen.

Aperture Priority AE Video Recording

In the Aperture priority mode for videos, choose the right aperture for your movie. The camera will automatically adjust ISO and shutter speed for the correct brightness.

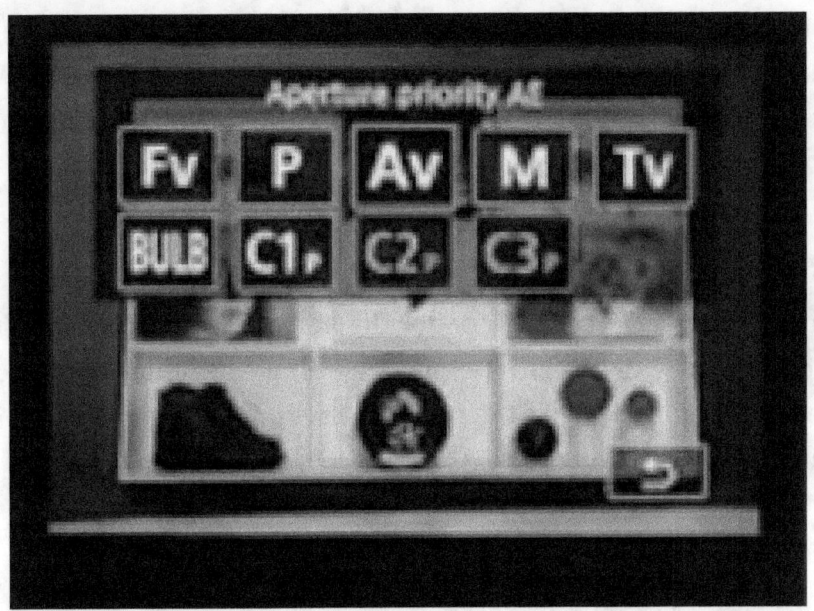

To set this mode:

1. Switch to video mode using the photo/movie switch.
2. Press the MODE dial.
3. On the next screen, turn the main dial to select Aperture-Priority AE and press SET.

Adjust the aperture value (1): Turn the big knob while watching the screen where you take pictures.

Focus on your subjects: Press the shutter button halfway to focus on the chosen area. You can use either Auto-focus or

Manual focus before recording a video. Normally, Movie Servo AF is on, so your camera will keep focusing on your subject.

Begin recording your video: Press the button to start filming. You can also begin recording by tapping the red dot on the screen. While recording, you'll see the REC icon at the top right. The camera's microphone will capture sound. To stop recording, press the movie button again or click the red square on the screen.

Manual Exposure Video Recording

In this setting, you get to decide how bright or dark your pictures or videos will be by adjusting the shutter speed, aperture, or ISO. It might be a bit tricky for beginners, so be careful when picking it.

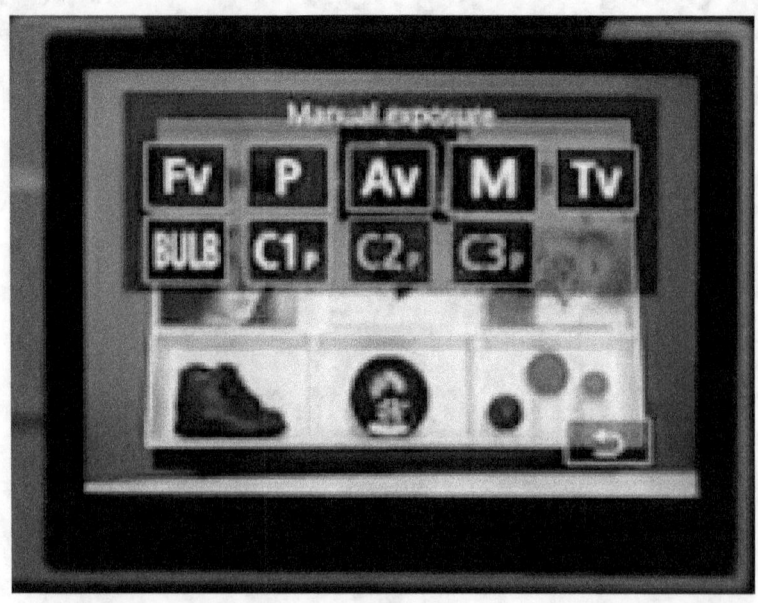

To use it:

1. Change the switch for taking photos or recording videos to video mode.
2. Turn the mode dial.
3. On the next screen, turn the main dial to select manual exposure recording and press the SET button.

Adjust the shutter speed: Turn the main dial as you watch the shooting screen. The shutter speeds you can use depend on the frame rate.

Adjust the aperture value: Turn the dial 1 on the camera while you're watching the screen where you take pictures.

Adjust the ISO speed: Turn the small dial to the right twice while checking the camera screen.

Focus on your subjects: Press the shutter button halfway to focus on the chosen area. Before recording a video, you can use Auto-focus or Manual focus. Typically, Movie Servo AF is on, ensuring your camera consistently focuses on the subject.

Begin recording your video: Press the button to start filming. You can also begin recording by tapping the red dot on the screen. While recording, you'll see the REC icon at the top right, and the camera's microphone will capture sound. To stop recording, press the movie button again or click the red square on the screen.

Movie Self Timer

You can begin filming by using the automatic self-timer.

Tap MENU to open your camera settings. Go to the Shooting menu tab, scroll to tab 6 with the Main dial, pick Movie self-timer, and press SET.

Turn the Quick control dial to choose Off, 10 sec, or 2 sec, and then press the SET button.

Press the movie shooting button or tap the red circle on the screen to begin recording a video. Your camera will display the remaining seconds and make a beeping sound.

Audio recording

You can make videos while capturing sound using the built-in or an external stereo microphone. You have the flexibility to adjust the recording volume. To activate the audio recording feature, follow these steps:

- Press the MENU button to open your camera settings. Go to the Shooting menu tab by turning the Main dial. Select shooting tab 1. Choose Sound Recording, and press the SET button.
- Turn the Quick control dial to choose either Sound recording, Wind filter, or Attenuator. Press the SET button.

Sound recording level

Choose Sound Recording: Go to your camera settings, find the Shooting menu, go to Shooting tab 1, pick Sound Recording, and press the SET button.

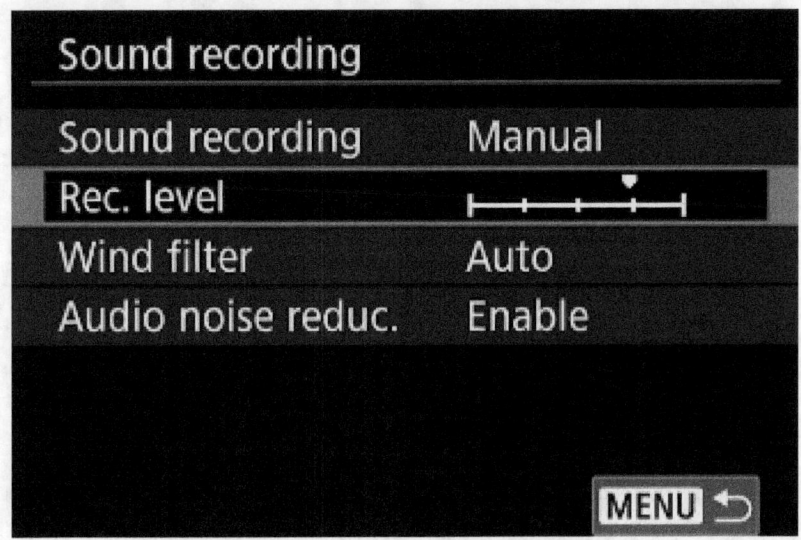

Choose Sound recording: Turn the Quick control dial to select "Sound recording" and then press the SET button.

Choose one option: Turn the Quick control dial 1 to choose an option, and then press the SET button.

- **Auto:** The volume is adjusted by itself. It changes based on how loud the sound is.
- **Manual:** Change the audio recording volume as you like. In step 2, pick Rec. level instead of Sound recording, and turn the Quick control dial to set the recording level while keeping an eye on the sound level meter. Pay attention to the peak hold indicator and adjust it so that the level meter occasionally lights up to the right of the "12" (-12 dB) max volume mark. If it goes above "0," the sound will distort.
- **Disable:** There is no audio recorded.

Wind filter

Choose Sound Recording: Go to your camera settings, open the Shooting menu, go to Shooting tab 1, pick Sound Recording, and press the SET button.

Choose Wind Filter: Turn the Quick control dial to select Wind Filter, then press the SET button.

Choose one option: Turn the Quick control dial to choose AUTO, Enable, or Disable, and then press the SET button.

Choose [Auto] to minimize noise in windy or noisy outdoor settings. This option turns off when you connect an external microphone to the external microphone IN terminal. Keep in mind that turning on the wind filter function will also reduce bass sounds.

Attenuator

When using the phone's microphone, this feature helps lower loud sounds.

Choose Sound Recording: Open your camera settings, go to the Shooting menu, select Shooting tab 1, choose Sound Recording, and press the SET button.

Choose Attenuator: Turn the Quick control dial 1 until "Attenuator" is selected. Press the SET button.

Choose one option: Turn the dial to choose High, Enable, or Disable on the Quick Control dial 1, then press the SET button.

- **Disable:** Turn off noise reduction.

- **Enable:** Turn on noise reduction.
- **High:** Reduces more audio noise than Enable.

CONCLUSION

The Canon EOS R3 is a powerful camera that can help you take amazing photos and videos. This guide has taught you everything you need to know to get started with the EOS R3, from setting up the camera to using its advanced features.

Whether you're a beginner or a seasoned photographer, the EOS R3 can help you take your skills to the next level. With its high-resolution sensor, fast autofocus system, and 4K video capabilities, the EOS R3 is a great camera for capturing any moment.

www.ingramcontent.com/pod-product-compliance
Lightning Source LLC
Chambersburg PA
CBHW062332290526
45794CB00005B/2009